T0301903

An Analysis of

Mary Douglas's

Purity and Danger:
An Analysis of Concepts
of Pollution and Taboo

Pádraig Belton

Published by Macat International Ltd
24:13 Coda Centre, 189 Munster Road, London SW6 6AW.

Distributed exclusively by Routledge
2 Park Square, Milton Park, Abingdon, Oxon OX14 4RN
711 Third Avenue, New York, NY 10017, USA

Routledge is an imprint of the Taylor & Francis Group, an informa business

www.macat.com
info@macat.com

Cataloguing in Publication Data
A catalogue record for this book is available from the British Library.
Library of Congress Cataloguing-in-Publication Data is available upon request.
Cover illustration: Kim Thompson

ISBN 978-1-912303-92-2 (hardback)
ISBN 978-1-912284-63-4 (paperback)
ISBN 978-1-912284-77-1 (e-book)

Notice
The information in this book is designed to orientate readers of the work under analysis,
to elucidate and contextualise its key ideas and themes, and to aid in the development
of critical thinking skills. It is not meant to be used, nor should it be used, as a
substitute for original thinking or in place of original writing or research. References and
notes are provided for informational purposes and their presence does not constitute
endorsement of the information or opinions therein. This book is presented solely for
educational purposes. It is sold on the understanding that the publisher is not engaged
to provide any scholarly advice. The publisher has made every effort to ensure that
this book is accurate and up-to-date, but makes no warranties or representations with
regard to the completeness or reliability of the information it contains. The information
and the opinions provided herein are not guaranteed or warranted to produce particular
results and may not be suitable for students of every ability. The publisher shall not be
liable for any loss, damage or disruption arising from any errors or omissions, or from
the use of this book, including, but not limited to, special, incidental, consequential or
other damages caused, or alleged to have been caused, directly or indirectly, by the
information contained within.

CONTENTS

THE MACAT LIBRARY

The Macat Library is a series of unique academic explorations of seminal works in the humanities and social sciences – books and papers that have had a significant and widely recognised impact on their disciplines. It has been created to serve as much more than just a summary of what lies between the covers of a great book. It illuminates and explores the influences on, ideas of, and impact of that book. Our goal is to offer a learning resource that encourages critical thinking and fosters a better, deeper understanding of important ideas.

Each publication is divided into three Sections: Influences, Ideas, and Impact. Each Section has four Modules. These explore every important facet of the work, and the responses to it.

This Section-Module structure makes a Macat Library book easy to use, but it has another important feature. Because each Macat book is written to the same format, it is possible (and encouraged!) to cross-reference multiple Macat books along the same lines of inquiry or research. This allows the reader to open up interesting interdisciplinary pathways.

To further aid your reading, lists of glossary terms and people mentioned are included at the end of this book (these are indicated by an asterisk [*] throughout) – as well as a list of works cited.

Macat has worked with the University of Cambridge to identify the elements of critical thinking and understand the ways in which six different skills combine to enable effective thinking.
Three allow us to fully understand a problem; three more give us the tools to solve it. Together, these six skills make up the **PACIER** model of critical thinking. They are:

ANALYSIS – understanding how an argument is built
EVALUATION – exploring the strengths and weaknesses of an argument
INTERPRETATION – understanding issues of meaning

CREATIVE THINKING – coming up with new ideas and fresh connections
PROBLEM-SOLVING – producing strong solutions
REASONING – creating strong arguments

To find out more, visit **WWW.MACAT.COM.**

CRITICAL THINKING AND *PURITY AND DANGER: AN ANALYSIS OF CONCEPTS OF POLLUTION AND TABOO*

Primary critical thinking skill: EVALUATION
Secondary critical thinking skill: REASONING

Mary Douglas is an outstanding example of an evaluative thinker at work. In *Purity and Danger: An Analysis of Concepts of Pollution and Taboo*, she delves in great detail into existing arguments that portray traditional societies as "evolving" from "savage" beliefs in magic, to religion, to modern science, then explains why she believes those arguments are wrong. She also adeptly chaperones readers through a vast amount of data, from firsthand research in the Congo to close readings of the Old Testament, and analyzes it in depth to provide evidence that religions in these contexts have more in common than the first comparative religion scholars and early anthropologists thought.

First evaluating her scholarly predecessors by marshalling their arguments, Douglas identifies their main weakness: that they dismiss traditional societies and their religions by identifying their practices as "magic," thereby creating a chasm between "savages" who believe in magic and "sophisticates" who practice religion.

Douglas's central theme is that religions in modern and traditional societies share vast areas of commonality. To prove this, she identifies the centrality of cleanliness in the conceptualization of taboos across a range of religions including African tribal faiths and Christianity. Building on the claim made by William James* and others that "dirt is matter out of place", Douglas goes on to argue that the concepts of filth and pollution are central to all social organization."

She reasons that common, cross-cutting concepts such as pollution and purity will mend the weakness she sees in prior comparative religion scholarship. By then examining in great detail a wide range of data about what constitutes dirt in different societies, she is able to identify aspects that are common to multiple religions, such as African tribal religions and Christianity.

This strong emphasis on evaluating the work of those who preceded her in the fields of anthropology and comparative religion, along with conducting her own detailed fieldwork on traditional peoples rather than simply rehearsing encyclopedic volumes of data, are defining features of Douglas's work.

ABOUT THE AUTHOR OF THE ORIGINAL WORK

British academic **Dame Mary Douglas** was one of the twentieth century's leading social scientists, known for her writings on human culture, symbolism, and how ideas of purity and defilement unite religions and other belief structures around the world. *Purity and Danger: An Analysis of Concepts of Pollution and Taboo* and her research in the Congo cemented her worldwide reputation, and she wrote for both wide public and academic audiences on topics ranging from risk to the Bible.

ABOUT THE AUTHOR OF THE ANALYSIS

Pádraig Belton was educated at Yale, Oxford, and the School of Oriental and African Studies. He has received a Fulbright fellowship and the Royal United Services Institute's Trench-Gascoigne Prize for writing in foreign affairs. A journalist, he contributes for the BBC, *Times Literary Supplement, Spectator,* and S&P's financial newswire.

ABOUT MACAT

GREAT WORKS FOR CRITICAL THINKING

Macat is focused on making the ideas of the world's great thinkers accessible and comprehensible to everybody, everywhere, in ways that promote the development of enhanced critical thinking skills.

It works with leading academics from the world's top universities to produce new analyses that focus on the ideas and the impact of the most influential works ever written across a wide variety of academic disciplines. Each of the works that sit at the heart of its growing library is an enduring example of great thinking. But by setting them in context – and looking at the influences that shaped their authors, as well as the responses they provoked – Macat encourages readers to look at these classics and game-changers with fresh eyes. Readers learn to think, engage and challenge their ideas, rather than simply accepting them.

'Macat offers an amazing first-of-its-kind tool for interdisciplinary learning and research. Its focus on works that transformed their disciplines and its rigorous approach, drawing on the world's leading experts and educational institutions, opens up a world-class education to anyone.'

Andreas Schleicher
Director for Education and Skills, Organisation for Economic Co-operation and Development

'Macat is taking on some of the major challenges in university education … They have drawn together a strong team of active academics who are producing teaching materials that are novel in the breadth of their approach.'

Prof Lord Broers,
former Vice-Chancellor of the University of Cambridge

'The Macat vision is exceptionally exciting. It focuses upon new modes of learning which analyse and explain seminal texts which have profoundly influenced world thinking and so social and economic development. It promotes the kind of critical thinking which is essential for any society and economy. This is the learning of the future.'

Rt Hon Charles Clarke, former UK Secretary of State for Education

'The Macat analyses provide immediate access to the critical conversation surrounding the books that have shaped their respective discipline, which will make them an invaluable resource to all of those, students and teachers, working in the field.'

Professor William Tronzo, University of California at San Diego

WAYS IN TO THE TEXT

KEY POINTS

* The British academic Mary Douglas was born Mary Tew in 1921, in San Remo, Italy, and grew up in England.

* Douglas's approach in *Purity and Danger* was unique because she developed a robust framework to link both Western and tribal systems of religion: each offers classification schemes that yield "matter out of place," which can be thought of in terms of "dirt" and "purity."

* Douglas argues that we should understand both "primitive" and "modern" beliefs in terms of comparing what is ordered and lawful to that which is "dirt"— unordered, dangerous, but also powerful.

Who Was Mary Douglas?

Born in 1921 in San Remo, Italy, as her parents traveled home from Burma (now Myanmar), Mary Douglas grew up in Devon, England, and at a Catholic convent school in London. She studied philosophy, politics, and economics at St. Anne's College, Oxford, and went from there to the British Colonial Office. Then she returned to Oxford in 1949 where she studied for a doctorate in anthropology,* coming under the influence of Professor (later Sir) E. E. Evans-Pritchard.*

Douglas's interest in anthropology began, she said, with her experience in the Colonial Office, where the social anthropologists* she met intrigued her. Her first field research was carried out in what was then the Belgian Congo (now the Democratic Republic of the Congo).

After earning her doctorate from Oxford University in 1952, Douglas became an academic, lecturing at University College London, where she was made a professor of social anthropology* from 1970 to 1977 and a distinguished fellow in 1994. She later worked in New York at the Russell Sage Foundation and taught at Northwestern University. She was also a visiting professor at Yale and Princeton universities.

Douglas and her husband, a civil servant, were known for their London dinner parties at which officials and academics would mix. In 2006, she was made a Dame, the female equivalent of a knight, for her contributions to society. She died later that year, aged 86. She remains one of the most widely read academics in social anthropology.

Douglas was principally interested in comparing "modern" and "primitive" societies and relating their ideas of hygiene and holiness. *Purity and Danger: An Analysis of Concepts of Pollution and Taboo* was her first book on the subject and her most influential, as well as an international best seller. Altogether she wrote 19 books, including texts examining cross-cultural perspectives on drinking and good taste.

Expanding on the ideas in *Purity and Danger* in her later work, Douglas sought other ways to compare Western and non-Western societies and used insights from her fieldwork about group membership, reconciliation, and risk to understand modern society. But she remains principally known for her work in *Purity and Danger*, which is taught as a key text at nearly every university in the world offering social anthropology and comparative religion classes. It is also cited by scholars working in an increasing number of other disciplines, such as economics and environmental studies.

What Does *Purity and Danger* Say?

Douglas's book first and foremost provides readers with a strong and valuable framework for comparing societies based on understanding what each group considers sacred, hygienic, and dirty.

This framework starts with the observation (which had been previously made by other writers, including William James*) that dirt is "matter out of place." For Douglas, all humans share a deep-seated desire to order their world, but all of these schemes of classification produce anomalies. This "matter out of place," whether humble house dust in her London home in Highgate, or animals that do not fit into the divisions of species in the Bible's Book of Leviticus,* is "dirt": that is, something that disrupts our sense of how the world should be. Sometimes these dirty things are seen as polluting, such as pigs in the Old Testament,* which share the cloven hoof of ungulates (hoofed mammals) but do not chew cud. Other times, however, so-called "dirty" things have had great power: Jesus of Nazareth,* a poor man born out of wedlock and killed as a common criminal, fell outside first-century Judea's* religious and civic categories of proper behavior, but for Christians* (and Douglas was a devout Catholic* in a family of distant Irish extraction), he became the embodiment of the sacred.

Likewise, Douglas describes how the Lele* people of the Congo, whom she first encountered in her doctoral fieldwork, relate to the pangolin*—an insect-eating mammal, some species of which live nocturnally in trees. For them, the pangolin does not fit into any of their frameworks: it has large, plate-like scales, but is not a fish, and it produces one child at a time, like humans. However, its rule-breaking character gives it tremendous power: For the Lele, the pangolin, when it is ritually slain, becomes a kingly victim that, by dying, releases great power. Its body is carried around the village after, as though it were a chief.

The paradox at the heart of *Purity and Danger,* then, is that our attempts to impose order inevitably fail. "Dirt" is always dangerous, and therefore powerful, and its defiance of the rules can provide the impetus to restart the system afresh and forge a new order.

Douglas argues that this is a common pattern across societies and religions. "That which is rejected is ploughed back for the renewal of life," she wrote in *Purity and Danger.*[1]

Douglas did not invent these categories of hygiene and purity or dirt and danger, nor was she the first to use them to understand Western and non-Western societies, but she did think about them in new, systematic ways that she suggests are easy to apply to a wide range of both traditional and modern societies.

Building on the turn-of-the-century ideas of Émile Durkheim,* who argued that religious ideas are embedded in social structures,* Douglas demonstrated in a new, clear way that this principle—which Durkheim applied only to "primitive" cultures—could also be applied to "modern" societies.*

Douglas's research has inspired many other scholars to look in new ways at many other aspects linking Western and non-Western ideas of religion and purity. She herself built on the masterful foundations of *Purity and Danger* in her 1970 book *Natural Symbols*, which explores such further questions as what types of society can produce the types of symbolism that forge the most meaningful life for their members.

Her astuteness in perceiving connections between Western Christianity and traditional beliefs, like those of the Lele, resonated with Douglas's wide range of readers, who include academics, journalists, and members of the general public.

Why Does *Purity and Danger* Matter?

It is hard to overstate the importance of *Purity and Danger*, which has been called "one of the most remarkable studies on faith ever written."[2] It has gone through eight editions and reprintings, and the *Times Literary Supplement* listed it as among the hundred most influential non-fiction books published since the World War II.*

Douglas's book is read as a key text in anthropology, sociology, and religious studies classrooms in universities around the world, and it has influenced the way scholars have looked at subjects from climate change, to dietary laws in the Hebrew Bible, to early Christian religious life. It is easily one of the most influential books in the sphere of comparative religion, anthropology, and cultural theory of the last 50 years.

Douglas described her predecessor, Durkheim, as one of the great discoverers of "the secret places of the mind."[3] Like Karl Marx*, Sigmund Freud,*, and Friedrich Nietzsche*, Durkheim showed that we are shaped by motives and dimensions of ourselves that are hidden from our ordinary awareness. But where Durkheim only focused on "exotic" and "primitive" non-Western societies, Douglas showed that the same insights applied to "modern"Western societies, too.

Understood and used properly, these categories of purity and dirt, propriety and inappropriateness, and safety and danger will help readers understand both their own and very different societies in a new, illuminating way.

Douglas also expanded these ideas in her later work with the political scientist Aaron Wildavsky* to explain how societies everywhere handle risk perception and manage conflicts over risk. This powerful framework yielded the new academic field of the cultural theory of risk, and has given rise to a broad set of research projects that span many fields of social science and have been used to explain conflicts over policymaking.

Among the awards Douglas received after writing *Purity and Danger* was the invitation to give the Gifford Lectures, one of the most important series of lectures in Scottish academia, in 1989. These lectures were the origin of her 1993 book *In the Wilderness*, which examines ideas of defilement in the Bible's Book of Numbers.* She was elected a Fellow of the British Academy and in 2006 was made a Dame, or female knight, one of the highest awards given by the Queen of England.

A half century after its publication, *Purity and Danger* remains indispensable reading for anyone interested in understanding the similarities between how modern and traditional societies treat the sacred and unclean, and in probing the concealed workings of all human societies the world over.

NOTES

1   Mary Douglas, *Purity and Danger: An Analysis of Concepts of Pollution and Taboo*, vol. 2 of *Mary Douglas: Collected Works* (Abingdon: Routledge, 2002), 168.

2   Tanya Luhrmann, "The Paradox of Donald Trump's Appeal," *Sapiens*, July 29, 2016, accessed December 3, 2017, https://www.sapiens.org/culture/mary-douglas-donald-trump/.

3   Mary Douglas, *Implicit Meanings: Essays in Anthropology* (London: Routledge & Kegan Paul, 1975), xx.

SECTION 1
INFLUENCES

MODULE 1
THE AUTHOR AND THE
HISTORICAL CONTEXT

KEY POINTS

- *Purity and Danger* ushered in a new way of understanding how all societies and groups deal with the everyday, the excluded, and the prohibited.

- Mary Douglas's childhood experience of the British Empire* and Catholic convent education exposed her to the importance of social structure in creating meaning in different cultures and geographical contexts.

- Since *Purity and Danger* was written, nearly every religion and anthropology student has been exposed to the principles in Douglas's book; it has deeply influenced how we understand groups, societies, and beliefs wherever they occur.

Why Read This Text?

Mary Douglas's impact on the way we understand human culture in both Western and non-Western societies is profound. The *Telegraph* described her as "perhaps the leading British anthropologist of the second half of the 20th century,"[1] while the *Guardian* called her "the most widely read British social anthropologist of her generation."[2] One magazine, *Commonwealth*, called Douglas "along with Clifford Geertz* perhaps the most influential social anthropologist from any background."[3]

But just because Douglas's key arguments about dirt, purity, and holiness are now nearly universally used does not mean they are always used properly. A question was asked in the British Parliament about

> 66 The individual human being, stripped of his humanity, is of no use as a conceptual base from which to make a picture of human society. No human exists except steeped in the culture of his time and place. 99
>
> Mary Douglas and Baron Isherwood, *The World of Goods*

funding social science research, with one member describing Douglas's work as "the sociology of the biscuit."[4] Many people in social sciences and elsewhere get these concepts second hand and end up with understandings that are both inaccurate and incomplete. Correctly understanding the powerful insights in *Purity and Danger: An Analysis of Concepts of Pollution and Taboo* and putting them into practice requires avoiding these misconceptions.

Reading *Purity and Danger* is key to correctly applying its most important concepts about human culture, whether in our own societies or ones that are very different. These include the ideas that all societies deal with their most important concepts, including holiness and ordering, through systems of classification; that all schemes of classification produce anomalies; and that some examples of "matter out of place" that result are polluting, but others have the capacity in a symbolic way to reset both the world view, and, by extension, the world. "Reflection on dirt," says Douglas, involves reflection on the relation of "order to disorder, form to formlessness, life to death."[5]

Author's Life

Mary Douglas (originally Margaret Mary Tew) was born in 1921 in San Remo, Italy. Her father was a member of the Indian Civil Service, and her family's involvement in the administration of the British Empire sparked her lifelong interest in the relationship between Western and non-Western societies. Returning to England from

Burma, where her father had been stationed, and from the age of five living with grandparents in Devon, she received a Roman Catholic convent education in London from the age of 12, further increasing her interest in religion and how Western societies create order, hierarchy, and belonging in daily life.

Academically, Douglas began as a student of philosophy, politics, and economics at St. Anne's College, Oxford, graduating in 1942. She then took this wide-ranging background to the United Kingdom Colonial Office, where she worked during World War II. This experience kindled an interest in academic anthropology, and she returned to Oxford in 1946 as a student of E. E. Evans-Pritchard, who had just arrived as a professor in the college's Institute of Social Anthropology.

Evans-Pritchard suggested that Douglas do fieldwork among the Lele of the then-Belgian Congo, and she submitted her doctorate on that research in 1953. In 1951, she became a lecturer at University College, London, where she remained for 20 years, and married her husband, a civil servant named James Douglas.

Douglas is best known for her work on systems of taboo, dirt, and people's need for classification, as well as her celebrated 1966 book *Purity and Danger*, which changed the thinking of a readership both within the academic world and far beyond it.

The ideas Douglas explores in *Purity and Danger* first emerged in her doctoral thesis on the Lele, which she published in 1963 as *The Lele of the Kasai*. She then continued to expand on the ideas in *Purity and Danger* in other books, notably *Natural Symbols*, published four years later, and *The World of Goods* in 1979. Altogether, she wrote 19 books and is widely considered the creator of the cultural theory explaining how societies deal with conflict over risk. She became professor of social anthropology at University College, London, and towards the end of her career, she spent 11 years in America, including three years at Princeton University.

The idea for *Purity and Danger* first arose, said Douglas, from the vast difference between her husband's more fastidious views on cleanliness and her own. "In matters of cleanness his threshold of tolerance is so much lower than my own that he more than anyone else has forced me into taking a stand on the relativity of dirt," she said in her book's preface.[6]

Author's Background

Douglas's early work pioneered understanding of the Lele of the Kasai, an African tribe in Congo, in a book that became a classic of anthropology and revealed that the Lele said things that uncannily recalled passages of the Old and New Testaments.* The pangolin (a scaly mammal similar to an anteater) was taboo, inedible, and dangerous, but also sacred for them. She said both the Lele and Jews* and Christians used ideas of a voluntary victim—the pangolin, Abraham's ram in the thicket, and Jesus of Nazareth—to express a transcendent understanding of the tragic facts of death.

In Britain and America, the 1960s were a time of economic expansion, but also of insecurity about the role of established hierarchies and social structures, which were challenged by people born after World War II ("baby boomers"*) as they entered university and formed student movements.* *Purity and Danger* offered an intellectual framework for understanding the value and functions of social structures as they were increasingly examined and called into question by broader society.

After writing *Purity and Danger*, Douglas further explored its ideas in her 1970 book *Natural Symbols* by considering what kinds of societies are best able to support complex symbolism and correlated structures of social organization with patterns of belief and morality. She concluded that institutions that are hierarchical, differentiated, and have clear boundaries offered the most promising environments for complex thinking and symbolism.

NOTES

1   *Telegraph*, "Dame Mary Douglas," May 22, 2007, accessed December 3, 2017, http://www.telegraph.co.uk/news/obituaries/1552231/Dame-Mary-Douglas.html.

2   Richard Fardon, "Dame Mary Douglas," *Guardian*, May 18, 2007, accessed December 3, 2017, https://www.theguardian.com/news/2007/may/18/guardianobituaries.obituaries.

3   John McGreevy, "Mary Douglas RIP," *Commonweal*, May 22, 2007, accessed December 3, 2017, https://www.commonwealmagazine.org/mary-douglas-rip.

4   "Professor Dame Mary Douglas, 1921-2007," *The Douglas Archives, accessed December 3, 2017, http://www.douglashistory.co.uk/history/marydouglas2.htm.*

5   Mary Douglas, *Purity and Danger: An Analysis of Concepts of Pollution and Taboo*, vol. 2 of *Mary Douglas: Collected Works* (Abingdon: Routledge, 2002), 6.

6   *Purity and Danger*, VIII.

MODULE 2
ACADEMIC CONTEXT

KEY POINTS

- British anthropological modernism* began after the ruin of World War I.* Heavily influenced by Émile Durkheim in France, who, like Sigmund Freud and Karl Marx, emphasized the role of forces beyond participants' conscious knowledge, it rejected Victorian* notions of evolution and progress in understanding society.

- Mary Douglas rejected the idea of her nineteenth-century British predecessors, William Robertson Smith* and James Frazer,* that magic is distinct from religion (which is more evolved). Following the example of her more recent predecessors Alfred Radcliffe-Brown* and E. E. Evans-Pritchard in Oxford, she strongly advocated systematic fieldwork and comparison of similarities across societies.

- Douglas saw herself as bridging the Anglo-American and Continental traditions in religious scholarship and using influences like Durkheim's to remedy shortcomings in English-language scholarship.

The Work In Its Context

Mary Douglas wrote in a modernist tradition within British anthropology, which, after the devastation of World War I, turned away from Victorian triumphalist ideas that saw human progress as a story of ascent from superstition to modern science. Instead, anthropological modernism looked at how all our systems of knowledge and morals are embedded in social structures that construct and constrain them. This tradition was largely influenced by Émile Durkheim, whose thinking influenced Douglas's own mentor at Oxford, E. E. Evans-Pritchard.

> ❝ The falsely abstracted individual has been sadly misleading to Western political thought. But now we can start again at a point where major streams of thought converge, at the other end, at the making of culture. Cultural analysis sees the whole tapestry as a whole, the picture and the weaving process, before attending to the individual threads. ❞
>
> Mary Douglas and Baron Isherwood, *The World of Goods*

For Douglas, the great "central task of philosophy in this century" is integrating Sigmund Freud's work on belief, Karl Marx and the scholarship he instigated on social structure, and Durkheim's insights into how our thoughts are entangled with our social environment.[1] She described these three figures as great modern discoverers of secret places of the mind who show we are shaped by forces beyond our awareness.

However, Douglas thought Durkheim did not go far enough in turning the anthropological gaze back upon ourselves, and he exempted modern Western culture from the entanglements of thought and social structure he found in traditional societies.

Accordingly, Douglas's personal project, as she described in a later essay, was "to bring anthropology to bear on the sources of our own civilization" in the Bible.[2] In Europe before the Enlightenment,* she said, other religions were condemned as false, even as evil, and after the Enlightenment as irrational superstition, but neither stance was conducive to understanding.

Anthropology, Douglas argued, should provide a critical, humane, and sensitive interpretation of other religions and show how they are linked to our own practices. Whether in the Congo or in London, it is impossible to have social relations without symbolic acts. For her, rules about purity, such as those in the Bible, set up "the great inclusive categories in which the whole universe is hierarchized and structured."[3]

Overview Of The Field

Douglas sought to unite insights from previous works by Continental and Anglo-American scholars in grounding the new discipline of social anthropology.

In Britain, William Robertson Smith, a Scottish Victorian academic, pioneered the use of sociology* in studying religious phenomena with his 1889 book *Religion of the Semites*, his most important work. He saw the ethical relationship of individuals with community gods as the center of religion, while magic had to do with rituals and the placation of terrible demons. James Frazer expanded upon this distinction between religion and magic in his wide-ranging 1890 comparative study of religion *The Golden Bough*, where he described old religions as fertility cults, revolving around worship and periodic sacrifice of a sacred king, and proposed that humanity progresses from magic, to religious belief, to scientific thought.

Douglas had utter contempt for Frazer, describing his influence "a baneful one."[4] She suggested rectifying his sharp distinction between primitive magic and modern religion by looking to Continental authors such as Claude Lévi-Strauss,* who in his books *Tristes Tropiques* (1955) and *The Savage Mind* (1962) argued that we should look for commonalities between people in traditional and modern societies, rather than distinguishing them as either "primitive" and "savage" or "civilized."

Also in the twentieth century, Mircea Eliade,* a Romanian professor at the University of Chicago, proposed that the basis of religion is to divide experience into sacred and profane. In profane times, people get on with daily life; but in sacred times, religious people participate in and commemorate manifestations of the sacred (which he called hierophanies*) that give the world value, direction, and purpose. Eliade's idea of hierophanies influenced Douglas, but she felt that his definition of religion as "belief in spiritual beings" was too narrow.[5]

Academic Influences

Instead of viewing traditional and modern religion as a tale of evolution, *Purity and Danger: An Analysis of Concepts of Pollution and Taboo* shifts the discussion to their commonalities. In so doing, it is influenced by (even if it begins to diverge from) the tradition of structural functionalism,* which views society as a complex system of cooperative parts, an approach that had begun to flourish in the Continent* in the late nineteenth century through the work of writers such as Émile Durkheim.

While empiricists* in the Anglo-American tradition such as David Hume* believe all realities in the outside world are the product of perception, for Durkheim and other functionalists, sociology could reveal the inherent nature of society. Durkheim placed great emphasis on establishing sociology as a science based on impartial observation and compared society to a living organism whose different parts were related and could each be explained by its function in maintaining the society's existence.

The British-born academic Alfred Radcliffe-Brown, who in 1937 was appointed to the first chair in social anthropology at Oxford College, was an important figure in importing this functionalist perspective into the English-speaking world. He rejected the evolutionary view of "primitive" and "modern" religion and argued for the use of rigorous fieldwork to compile lists of regularities in human societies and thus build up a genuinely scientific approach to understanding social life. To this end, he founded Oxford's Institute of Social and Cultural Anthropology, and in addition to bringing Durkheim into Anglo-American academia, he also developed a battery of concepts about how to conduct detailed ethnographic* field research.

Douglas's personal influence in this tradition was her mentor and doctoral supervisor, E. E. Evans-Pritchard, a fellow of All Souls College who started out expanding Radcliffe-Brown's program of functional research with three detailed works about the nomadic Nuer* pastoralists of contemporary South Sudan.

Evans-Pritchard's views of how accusations, blame, and responsibility are deployed through culturally specific concepts of misfortune and harm influenced Douglas's views on pollution, risk, and uncertainty. His 1965 book *Theories of Primitive Religion* was highly influential, arguing that anthropologists rarely entered the mindsets of the people they studied, and so ascribed to them motivations more closely matching the observers themselves and their culture.

NOTES

1   Mary Douglas, *Implicit Meanings: Essays in Anthropology* (London: Routledge & Kegan Paul, 1975), xx.

2   Mary Douglas, "Why I Have to Learn Hebrew: The Doctrine of Sanctification," *The Comity and Grace of Method: Essays in Honor of Edmund F. Perry*, eds. T. Ryba, G. D. Bond, and H. Tull (Evanston: Northwestern University Press, 2004), 151.

3   Jacob Neusner, *Idea of Purity in Ancient Judaism* (Leiden and Boston: Brill Academic Publishers, 1973), 138.

4   Mary Douglas, *Purity and Danger: An Analysis of Concepts of Pollution and Taboo*, vol. 2 of *Mary Douglas: Collected Works* (Abingdon: Routledge, 2002), 28.

5   Mircea Eliade, *Shamanism: Archaic Techniques of Ecstasy*, trans. Willard Trask (Princeton, N.J.: Princeton University Press, 2004), xiii.

MODULE 3
THE PROBLEM

KEY POINTS

- Victorian scholars such as James Frazer tried to look for unifying concepts across ancient and modern religions from around the world, though they ordinarily did not conduct field research, and they viewed religion through an evolutionary lens.

- Mary Douglas, drawing on the theoretical influence of Émile Durkheim and her own field research among the Lele in the Congo, identified dirt and purification as a unifying theme that did not view some religions as "primitive" and others as "advanced."

- In looking at how society spatially orders what is "dirty," Douglas asked questions similar to those posed by two Continental contemporaries, Henri Lefebvre* and Michel Foucault,* while her attempts to analyze her own society anticipated the "postmodern turn"* of scholars like James Clifford.*

Core Question

In *Purity and Danger: An Analysis of Concepts of Pollution and Taboo*, Mary Douglas asks what common trait can unite traditional and modern religious systems, not to mention other belief systems that are more contemporary. She presents this as an urgent task because she wishes to disprove the view, put forth by James Frazer and earlier scholars of religion, that "primitive" religions have been replaced in a process of evolution by more "advanced" ones—a stance she finds dismissive and distasteful.

❝ If we can abstract pathogenicity and hygiene from our notion of dirt, we are left with the old definition of dirt as matter out of place. This is a very suggestive approach. It implies two conditions: a set of ordered relations and a contravention of that order. Dirt, then, is never a unique, isolated event. ❞

Mary Douglas, *Purity and Danger*

Douglas also aims to bolster anthropology as a true social science in the tradition of Émile Durkheim and her functionalist mentors at Oxford, including E. E. Evans-Pritchard, by identifying interesting generalizations that are broadly valid across a wide range of societies.

Douglas is therefore happy that she has found what she believes to be a common trait uniting very disparate religions and belief systems: how societies treat pollution, corruption, and dirt.[1] Pollution symbols, she says, are as necessary as the use of black in any drawing, and so corruption can always be found enshrined in sacred places and times.

Douglas argues that reflecting on dirt—for example, what constitutes dirt, how it is managed, and what it means to be polluted— provides important insight into the different relations between various forms of structure and structurelessness: order and disorder, life and death, form and formlessness, being and non-being.

This concept of dirt serves as a tool for understanding society, providing insight into belief systems as wide-ranging as indigenous African religions, Catholicism, and the environmental movement. In particular, dirt in all these systems is not an aberration, but rather a part of the central project, needing to be purified. In these processes of purification, atonement is symbolically created and displayed, creating a "unity in experience" that Douglas calls the "central project of religion."[2]

It is these tools that Douglas tries to provide in *Purity and Danger*. She asks, how can we identify and understand what corresponds to "dirt" in different systems of belief—and having found what that particular system considers polluting, in what ways do its adherents tidy and creatively reorder their environment? These are the core questions of *Purity and Danger.*

The Participants

Prior to Douglas, others, including William James* and Henry Temple, Third Viscount Palmerston,* had articulated what seems to have been a common aphorism: that dirt is "matter out of place" (Douglas notes that William James uses it in *The Varieties of Religious Experience.*[3])

In *Purity and Danger,* there are two key scholarly participants. One is the Victorian Scottish social anthropologist Sir James Frazer, a longtime fellow at Trinity College, Cambridge. In 1890, Frazer wrote *The Golden Bough,* an early classic of comparative religion that depicts human belief as progressing through three stages, from primitive magic, through to religion, and ultimately to science. Like Douglas, his aim was to discover unifying principles for classical and contemporary religions from across the globe.

Though Frazer did not himself conduct field research apart from visits to Italy and Greece, he poured over ancient histories and sent questionnaires by post to missionaries and British Empire officials around the world. Douglas said "it is hard to forgive Frazer for his complacency and undisguised contempt of primitive society," adding he "perpetuated an ill-conceived division between religion and magic" where he viewed religion as further evolved than the "magic" practiced by indigenous peoples.[4]

Émile Durkheim, a French academic at Sorbonne University in Paris who was one of the founders of modern sociology, viewed religion as humanity's fundamental social institution that gave rise to the others. Like Frazer, he attempted to identify links between religions in different cultures. Though his theoretical contributions remain relevant, he has been criticized for taking his information on traditional religion from traders and missionaries rather than conducting field research himself.

In addition to these scholars, key participants in Douglas's story also include the Lele people themselves, of whom there are currently about 30,000 living in the Democratic Republic of Congo. Traditionally they live in the region of the Kasai River in the country's southwest, though in the last 50 years there has been heavy migration to Kinshasa, the country's capital and largest city. Also called the Bashilele* or Usilele,* they are organized matrilineally and believe in one god, Njambi, as well as other spiritual beings, and partake in several village cults whose members have particular spiritual authority and knowledge.

The pangolin cult, for example, which provided the basis for many of Douglas's insights about dirt, danger, and power, is reserved for male members of the Lele who had fathered a son and daughter with the same wife. Douglas wrote about the Lele in her doctoral thesis and her 1963 book based upon it, *The Lele of the Kasai.* The end of Belgian colonial rule in 1960 led to the Congo Crisis,* a civil war from 1960 to 1965 that influenced Douglas's decision to develop her scholarship along more theoretical lines rather than pursue further fieldwork. Many years later, the secretary of the Lele Community in the United Kingdom, Guillaume Iyenda,* delivered an address at Douglas's funeral on behalf of the Lele people.

The Contemporary Debate

Contemporary work in anthropology tends to place a great deal of importance on field research of the sort Douglas practiced in Africa and regard scholars like Frazer as "armchair anthropologists"* for working with material gathered by others.

The influence of contemporary scholars such as James Clifford, for many years a professor at the University of California, Santa Cruz, has led anthropology to take a "postmodern turn" which aims to be more acutely aware of the influence of the observer's class, race, gender, or cultural background on the scholarship they produce. Douglas's argument that the same patterns found in traditional religion can also be used to understand our own belief systems might be seen as leading up to this postmodern approach.

The way order and disorder are arranged in space is a vibrant question for scholarship today, where Douglas's influence is strongly felt along with the impact of two of her contemporaries in the late twentieth century on the Continent, Henri Lefebvre and Michel Foucault. Foucault investigated spaces such as hospitals, asylums, and prisons where society places those whose behavior is outside the norm and places like boarding schools and motel rooms where activities such as coming of age and honeymoons can take place out of sight. (He called such places heterotopias,* where undesirable bodies can be placed in order to make a utopian space possible elsewhere.) Lefebvre focused on how different types of societies manufacture space, which he saw as a social product. Contemporary scholars examining social and spatial processes of exclusion and disparagement frequently use Douglas's concepts alongside those of Foucault and Lefebvre. Another social theorist whose scholarship was shaped by Douglas was Zymunt Baumann*, who extended her ideas to examine how modern societies marginalize refugees, the homeless, and the unemployed.

Dirt, after Douglas, remains a lively topic of debate even today. Social geographers* use her concept of dirt to explore medical buildings, dumps, sewers, and cemeteries, as well as urban zoning and the repurposing of ex-industrial buildings. These researchers are following Douglas's lead in applying her theory broadly. Douglas herself put her simple but powerful characterization of belief systems around dirt and purity to work in explaining subjects as wide ranging as humor, consumer behavior, kosher dietary laws, and environmentalism.

NOTES

1   For example, Mary Douglas, *Purity and Danger: An Analysis of Concepts of Pollution and Taboo*, vol. 2 of *Mary Douglas: Collected Works* (Abingdon: Routledge, 2002), 29 and 33.

2   Douglas, *Purity and Danger*, 3.

3   Douglas, *Purity and Danger*, 165.

4   Douglas, *Purity and Danger*, 24, 28.

MODULE 4
THE AUTHOR'S CONTRIBUTION

KEY POINTS

- In *Purity and Danger*, Mary Douglas sets out to construct a general theory of how purity concepts work, offering a framework to compare how religions deal with pollution. One of her aims is to show identical processes at work in religions that earlier generations had characterized as either "savage" or "civilized."

- Douglas argues that ritual is to society what words are to thought and that religion cannot be understood apart from looking at society as a whole.

- Douglas uses Émile Durkheim's concept of sacred contagion* to explain how uncleanliness—which she defines as not fitting the categories constructed by society—can be passed from thing to person and vice versa.

Author's Aims

When she wrote *Purity and Danger: An Analysis of Concepts of Pollution and Taboo* in 1966, Mary Douglas had been lecturing at University College London for 15 years. Her book on her fieldwork (conducted between 1949 and 1953) with the Lele of the Congo had been greeted by warm reviews two years earlier. Her close field research and skill at documenting this matrilineal tribe and its complex marriage relationships, system of rule by elders (gerontocracy*), and religious cults established her reputation as an anthropologist.

However, because of its collapse into civil war, she would not be able to return to the Congo until 1987. Instead of continuing her field

> 66 Where there is dirt there is a system. Dirt is the by-product of a systematic ordering and classification of matter, in so far as ordering involves rejecting inappropriate elements. 99
>
> Mary Douglas, *Purity and Danger*

research, she delved next into theory to correct approaches by earlier authors she felt were seriously lacking. To start, she used her research on pollution among the Lele to look at pollution in very different contexts, such as the dietary rules of the Bible's Book of Leviticus.

Douglas refused to define "religion" (and criticized other authors, like Mircea Eliade, for doing so too narrowly), and instead set out to very broadly "compare people's views about man's destiny and place in the universe."[1]

In *Purity and Danger*, Douglas aims to provide a body of research to show a commonality between African tribesmen and liberal London housewives, following Claude Lévi-Strauss, who had already questioned the categorization of people and societies as "savage" and "civilized." As Douglas argues, what constitutes dirt is in flux—it is different in different contexts of geography and history—but the idea of "dirt" itself and our reactions to it are constant.

By using a framework that takes account of this constant role of dirt (however defined) in every society, Douglas demonstrates broad patterns linking societies in Africa and Europe, and—if one accepts her view that there is no such thing as dirt without classification—similarities in how they create and preserve order as well.

Approach

For Douglas, ritual is creative. It creates harmonious worlds with ranked and orderly populations playing their appointed parts and creates social realities. Rituals are to society, Douglas says, what words are to thought. Even money, she argues, is only an extreme and specialized form of ritual.

For Douglas, like Émile Durkheim, religion cannot be understood apart from society as a whole. In *Purity and Danger*, she attempts to show the relationship between behaviors around dirt and pollution in particular cultures and other detailed aspects of the same societies.

The human body, says Douglas, is the most apt symbol for society, and its functions can be seen as symbols of order and disorder in the entire society. Since danger attaches at the margins of society, pollution beliefs attach to the excretions coming out of the margins of the body. "The anxiety about bodily margins expresses danger to group survival," she says.[2]

Her approach here owes a great deal to the *Gestalt* school,* which takes its name from a German word for an organized whole greater than the sum of its parts. An important figure in this approach is Edward Sapir,* an American anthropologist and linguist who wrote his most important work in the 1930s and encouraged others to look at organized patterns (such as the relations of pollution or religious practices to power relationships) rather than "tiny tables of contents" (such as looking at religious practices on their own).

In her approach, Douglas also draws from her mentor E. E. Evans-Pritchard and his insights into the allocation of responsibility for misfortune as well as from Franz Steiner* and his ideas of taboo,* to which she adds an emphasis on the energy lurking in the margins and unstructured areas.

Contribution In Context

Douglas's approach in *Purity and Danger* draws heavily from, and develops extensively, the concept of sacred contagion: that spiritual properties of a person or object may be passed to another by contact or proximity.

Durkheim introduces this concept in *The Elementary Forms of Religious Life* and uses it to explain the Book of Leviticus. This book of the Bible, in Chapters 11 through 15, not only specifies which animals (as well as people, in states such as after menstruation) are clean and unclean, but also how that uncleanliness may be passed on to other persons or objects indefinitely.

Douglas expands this concept by adding the idea that animals forbidden under kosher dietary restrictions (also called kashrut*) are precisely those that fall between categories. All systems of classification (such as into ruminants*—animals that chew their cud and have cloven hoofs) generate "dirt" that does not fit its categories. In other words, every rule generates an exception. Pigs, which have split hoofs but do not chew their cud, are one example.

There have been many other attempts at explaining the passages in Leviticus that do not rely on this concept of sacred contagion. A different view, put forward by British Old Testament scholar Gordon Wenham,* is that such restrictions were meant to maintain a distinct Jewish identity by complicating socialization and intermarriage with those observing different dietary rules.

In contrast, Moses Maimonides,* the medieval physician and Jewish philosopher, in his chief work *Guide to the Perplexed*, argues a medical rationale behind the forbidden animals, saying their meat is difficult to digest. (This viewpoint has become known as medical materialism*.)

Finally, American anthropologist Marvin Harris,* who taught at the University of Florida, argued that pigs require water and shady woods with seeds, which are scarce resources in the Middle East. A similar argument is made by Richard Redding,* who suggests that chicken provides more nutrition and is more portable, hence the religious prohibition on pork.[3]

NOTES

1   Mary Douglas, *Purity and Danger: An Analysis of Concepts of Pollution and Taboo*, vol. 2 of *Mary Douglas: Collected Works* (Abingdon: Routledge, 2002), 29.

2   *Purity and Danger*, 125.

3   Richard W. Redding, "The Pig and the Chicken in the Middle East: Modeling Human Subsistence Behavior in the Archaeological Record Using Historical and Animal Husbandry Data," *Journal of Archaeological Research* 23, no. 4 (March 13, 2015): 325.

SECTION 2
IDEAS

MODULE 5
MAIN IDEAS

KEY POINTS

- Mary Douglas argues that all social groups have ideas about dirtiness and defilement, but we are socially conditioned to see certain things as dirt. All dirt is matter out of place, but not all matter out of place is dirt.

- Ritual acts, like the !Kung* rain dance or a Roman Catholic praying the Rosary* for a special intention, are not simply about manipulating future events, but involve imposing a sense of just order on the world.

- The world does not occasionally disappoint these expectations of just order; it does so inevitably. Religions from Catholicism to the cults of the Lele of the Congo use the dangerous, rule-breaking power of a "dirty" object, like the pangolin or the Crucifixion,* to reset the system.

Key Themes

One theme Mary Douglas powerfully expresses in *Purity and Danger: An Analysis of Concepts of Pollution and Taboo* is that although virtually all social groups have ideas about dirtiness and defilement, there is no such thing as absolute dirt.[1] Our perceptions about what is dirty are partly material and partly metaphorical, and they are strongly conditioned by linked physical states and social codes. If all dirt is matter out of place, the reverse is emphatically not true: not all matter out of place is dirt.

A second key theme in *Purity and Danger* is Douglas's attempt to overturn the lofty view, espoused by James Frazer in *The Golden Bough* and shared by many Victorians and Edwardians* in the nineteenth and early twentieth centuries, that secular post-Enlightenment societies*

> **"** Reflection on dirt involves reflection on the relation
> of order to disorder, being to non-being, form to
> formlessness, life to death. Wherever ideas of dirt are
> highly structured their analysis discloses a play upon
> such profound themes. This is why an understanding of
> rules of purity is a sound entry to comparative religion. **"**
>
> Mary Douglas, *Purity and Danger*

sat atop an ineluctable ladder of human development, a place reached
by societies that had passed through infatuations with magic and
religion.[2]

To argue against this view, Douglas recounts a story of
anthropologists studying a group of !Kung Bushmen who live in small
groups of 10 to 30 people surrounding bodies of water in the Kalahari
Desert,* which covers much of Botswana and some of Namibia and
South Africa.[3] The !Kung performed rain rituals, after which rain fell.
Subsequently, these anthropologists asked the !Kung if they believed
the rite had produced the rain, whereupon the Bushmen doubled up
laughing at the researchers' naïveté.

The !Kung simultaneously did and did not believe the rain rituals
actually worked: they held, at the same time, a conviction that events
would unfold as their faith said, and an awareness they might not. This
is not so dissimilar, Douglas argues, to a Roman Catholic praying for
assistance on a test or the remission of a disease; it is not false belief, but
rather touches upon her third theme, that ritual acts are not simply
about practical efficacy and manipulating future events, but involve
imposing a sense of just order on the world.

However, the world does not *occasionally* disappoint our
expectations that it be good, safe, and beautiful; it *inevitably* does so. For
this reason, says Douglas, religions from Catholicism to the faith of the
Lele often use the dangerous, rule-breaking power of a deeply "dirty"

object to reset the system. This may be the pangolin, or it may be Christ in the Crucifixion.

Exploring The Ideas

Where there is dirt, Douglas says, there is system. She sees in purity laws signs of an all-encompassing system of thought, in which more often than not the body becomes the paper on which ideas of society and the cosmos are written.

Far from being relics of primitive tribal superstition, then, purity rites are not to be treated with disdain but understood as part of expressive symbolic systems.

Douglas aims these arguments largely against Frazer as her principal *bête noire* (someone whose work she particularly dislikes). Émile Durkheim, however, also sharply distinguishes "primitive tribal cultures" (where all members know each other, and which have what he calls mechanical solidarity*) from modern Western cultures (with a greater population and division of labor, and so-called organic solidarity*).

For Durkheim, it is only in the social environments of traditional cultures where participants' thoughts, habits, and categories are closely entangled in ways of which they are largely unaware; he exempts modern societies. Douglas revokes this exemption, and, influenced by Sigmund Freud and Karl Marx, believes that in the secret places of the mind, all of us, traditional or modern, are shaped by forces beyond our conscious knowledge and will.

Eradicating this distinction between tribal and Western cultures is an important step to being able to turn the anthropological gaze upon ourselves. In this, Douglas is an important precursor to the focus in anthropology today following the postmodern turn* that prioritizes individual experience, relativism, and plural truths. Where social science in the age of Marx and Freud tried to build all-encompassing objective systems, scholarship after the rise of postmodernism has more often looked to uncover and explain what people in particular contexts believe to be true.

Language And Expression

Douglas's prose is always clear and accessible; readers may not necessarily agree with her argument, but they will always know what she means. For a researcher who served in the British government during wartime, grew up in a family employed in the British Empire, and spent 16 months in fieldwork living with the Lele, Douglas's metaphors are remarkably homely and emphatically ordinary, full of domestic references to shoes, lavatories, and cooking utensils. With her many references to household life in London, Douglas makes subtly but pointedly clear that concepts of dirt in contemporary Western society parallel traditional societies' own pollution practices.

She also (and here in pointed contrast to Durkheim, who was an atheist) always wrote about religion with sympathy, whether describing the cults of the Lele or dietary prohibitions in the Book of Leviticus. In addition to affecting her language, this also affected her treatment of the subject, as she argued that seemingly very different groups have religious experiences that are shaped by similar rules.

Douglas's imagination is deeply metaphorical, and ritual, for her, is also a sort of language where the body provides the words and broader society the meaning. Openings of the body, and objects that might enter or issue from the body, for her reflect dangers to the group's survival. Rituals that have to do with bodily margins and excreta, she says, are a language that should be interpreted as being about the boundaries of the group, the social organism.

NOTES

1   Mary Douglas, *Purity and Danger: An Analysis of Concepts of Pollution and Taboo*, vol. 2 of *Mary Douglas: Collected Works* (Abingdon: Routledge, 2002), 2.

2   Frazer, James George, *The Golden Bough. A Study in Magic and Religion. Part 1: The Magic Art and the Evolution of Kings, Vol. 1* (London: The Macmillan Press. [1906] 1976), ix.

3   *Purity and Danger*, 59.

MODULE 6
SECONDARY IDEAS

KEY POINTS

- Mary Douglas disagrees with Moses Maimonides, who argued that kosher dietary laws were motivated by health concerns, and the view that the laws only have a social function in distinguishing between members and non-members of the group. Instead, she argues, like Émile Durkheim, that every religion is at the same time a morality, a classification, and a cosmology.

- Ritual, for Douglas, externalizes individual experience and can both express and modify perceptual experience. Her broad definition of ritual includes money.

- An overlooked part of Douglas's thinking is that literal trash and rubbish, so long as it is in its place, is not dirt.

Other Ideas

In addition to her important theoretical contributions about dirt and order, Mary Douglas's detailed arguments in *Purity and Danger: An Analysis of Concepts of Pollution and Taboo* about Biblical restrictions around food and the religion of the Lele have also both been influential.

For Douglas, the Jewish kosher dietary laws expressed in the Old Testament's Book of Leviticus are not ancient health regulations or arbitrarily chosen membership rules to regulate who is inside and outside the group—though each perspective had been suggested by earlier authors.

Moses Maimonides interpreted Judaism*'s dietary laws as health guidelines, while Émile Durkheim explained such boundary-maintenance activities as a way to confirm group belonging and

> **❝** Social rituals create a reality which would be nothing without them. It is not too much to say that ritual is more to society than words are to thought. For it is very possible to know something and then find words for it. But it is impossible to have social relations without symbolic acts. **❞**
>
> Mary Douglas, *Purity and Danger*

purpose, while also serving an important function in rescuing group members from rootlessness, which he calls anomy.*

Douglas's answer, however, differs from both of these approaches, though it closely embodies Durkheim's maxim that every religion at the same time is a classification, a cosmology, and a morality. She identifies the animals Israelites* must not eat as the system's "dirt" (this is a question of morality), which does not fall into the broad sets of creatures (classifications) that inhabit, respectively, the air, sea, and land (cosmology). Examples she gives are marine animals which lack scales or fins (a category which includes eels and worms), four-footed creatures which fly or walk on their front hands (in the latter category she includes weasels, mice, and crocodiles), or terrestrial animals which creep, crawl, or swarm.[1]

A second subject to which Douglas gives lengthy treatment is the pangolin, a scaly anteater that she argues is both inedible and powerful because it does not fit within the Lele's classification system. The pangolin has scales, but is not a fish; it produces one offspring at a time, like humans normally do; it looks as though it should be in the water, but climbs up trees towards the sky; and, according to the Lele, it bows its head in the presence of its mother-in-law, like a human male.

But because of its in-between status, simultaneously associated with water, earth, and air, and sharing attributes of humanity, the pangolin is the perfect mediator between these natural categories and between nature and human culture. Being beyond categorization—outside the system—the pangolin has power that it can release by its decision (which Douglas describes as voluntary and kingly) to offer itself to be eaten.

Exploring The Ideas

Douglas's decision to apply the interpretive skills of modern anthropology (such as her insights from the Lele) to Biblical texts (such as Leviticus) is unremarkable now, but in the 1960s, it was a radical move.

Since Douglas viewed the texts of the Bible as the sources of her own Western civilization, treating Jewish dietary laws with the same analytical tools as the pangolin, for her, served the purposes of complicating the nineteenth-century dichotomy between "primitive" and "modern" modes of thought that she found so objectionable.

Such a comparison also reveals a cognitive and performative force uniting the rituals found in both. Ritual for her is not about magic, but about externalizing individual experience. Working on an individual's perceptions at a symbolic level, ritual can also modify a person's experience while expressing it and be a source of catharsis.*

Ritual for Douglas is not only "magic" practiced by primitives as technology, such as dances to bring about rain (the !Kung, in fact, view their rain dance in a similar way to how Christians view prayer). The days of the week constitute rituals, Douglas argues, as does money. Days of the week create experiences of time—what Sunday feels like compared to Monday—that would not be possible if we did not have them. It forms a part of human society and experience that is essential in framing and focusing attention and enlivening memory by linking the present with relevant bits of the past. She describes money as a ritual as well: like any ritual, it requires public confidence to be effective, mediates experiences, measures value, and links the present to the past and future.

Some may wonder if this doesn't broaden the concept of ritual so much that it ceases to be useful, even while sympathizing with Douglas's aim, which is to expand the purview of the concept in order to argue against the view that "foreigners know no true religion."[2]

Overlooked

Purity and Danger is chiefly known and referred to for the concepts described up to this point—dirt as a classificatory anomaly and as a cross-cutting analytical principle to use in rendering traditional and modern beliefs intelligible. For all her influence, Douglas does, though, provide a good many other insights which are largely overlooked.

Dirt and pollution for Douglas presume social order as the other side of the coin. Examples of pollution, then, require identifying corresponding weak points in the social order that need to be defended against, because, for Douglas, these are the precise points where pollution concepts operate. Often these examples of pollution are in the body, as the human body for Douglas is a strong metaphor for the social body. This analogy is crucial to her understanding of particular rituals among the Lele and other African tribes.

This is an area of Douglas's thinking that is very important in her system but largely ignored by those who apply her concepts. Douglas identifies four types of social dangers. One of these dangers is when the external boundaries of the system might be breached (war or invasion); another is when the internal lines of the system might be transgressed (such as gender roles); a third includes marginal cases (she gives the example of unborn children that are a danger because they are neither dead nor alive, and are neither known yet to be male nor female); and the fourth danger is contradictions between different parts of the system when it is at war with itself (such as intergenerational conflict). All of them may, and generally do, manifest themselves in rituals involving the body, Douglas argues. If she is correct, then this offers a powerful key for decoding the meaning behind a broad range of ritual behaviors.

It is paradoxical that Douglas's work has been so frequently used by scholars examining the representation of garbage in art, literature, and culture more broadly (an area known as discard studies), given that she herself was quite clear that garbage and dirt were not the same thing. The discard studies scholar Max Liboiron* noted garbage "does not even create ambiguous perceptions since it clearly belongs in a defined place, a rubbish heap of one kind or another."[3] *Waste: A Philosophy of Things* explicitly disputes the applicability of Douglas's definition to garbage, as do two other recent books, *Consumerism, Waste and Re-use in Twentieth-century Fiction*, and *Waste: An Object Lesson*.[4]

NOTES

1   Mary Douglas, *Purity and Danger: An Analysis of Concepts of Pollution and Taboo*, vol. 2 of *Mary Douglas: Collected Works* (Abingdon: Routledge, 2002), pp. 55-56.

2   Mary Douglas, *Purity and Danger*, p. 59.

3   Max Liboiron, "Discard Studies as Science and Technology Studies (STS)" (blog), *Discard Studies,* October 16, 2013, accessed December 3, 2017, https://discardstudies.com/2013/10/16/discard-studies-as-science-and-technology-studies-sts/.

4   William Viney, *Waste: A Philosophy of Things*, London: Bloomsbury, 2014; Rachele Dini, *Consumerism, Waste, and Re-Use in Twentieth-Century Fiction: Legacies of the Avant-Garde*, New York: Palgrave Macmillan, 2016; Brian Thill, *Waste: An Object Lesson*, London: Bloomsbury, 2015.

MODULE 7
ACHIEVEMENT

KEY POINTS

- Mary Douglas's project in *Purity and Danger* is Durkheimian,* which is to say it looks to how beliefs are socially constructed and the social function they serve.

- Knowledge, for Douglas, is contextual and depends on social and perceptual framing: An object is not out of place because it is dirty, but it is dirty *because* it is out of place.

- When Douglas wrote *Purity and Danger* in 1966, anthropology (which previously was highly associated with colonialism*) was in a crisis of confidence due to decolonization.* Douglas suggests that scientifically uncovering universally valid generalizations, a task she demonstrates, is a new and better approach for the discipline.

Assessing The Argument

In *Purity and Danger: An Analysis of Concepts of Pollution and Taboo*, Mary Douglas cleverly applies to something as common and omnipresent as dirt, disorder, and mess a framework for how the social order ritually renews and rejuvenates itself. It is a project that is essentially Durkheimian in the way it looks to the social origin and function of beliefs. She offers an analytic tool, dirt, which is at the same time broadly applicable (it is everywhere) and hugely interesting (it tells us important things about our societies).

This argument, and the deft work she makes of deploying it in both Biblical and African contexts, make the book justifiably a classic work. But there are still questions readers might raise in assessing it; here are three as examples.

❝ Uncomfortable facts which refuse to be fitted in, we find ourselves ignoring or distorting so that they do not disturb these established assumptions ... But it is not always an unpleasant experience to confront ambiguity ...There is a whole gradient on which laughter, revulsion and shock belong at different points and intensities.The experience can be stimulating. ❞

Mary Douglas, *Purity and Danger*

For one, Douglas's *Purity and Danger* is mainly known for her two detailed studies of Jewish dietary law and the pangolin cult of the Lele. Both pork and pangolin are forbidden, Douglas argues, because they fall outside classificatory frameworks. The pangolin is powerful and can release its power for good; but why not pork also? It does not seem to occur to Douglas to ask.

Second, though Douglas criticizes authors such as James Frazer for making broad distinctions between "primitive" and "modern" people, she herself draws a seemingly similar distinction between unified and compartmentalized experience. But is this to let in the same distinction by the back door?

Third, another question that might be asked is whether Douglas has defined "ritual" so broadly as to be meaningless. A related question is whether she confuses "ritual" with "mediation." Relationships are always a matter of mediation (e-mail and text messages, conversations), and mediation may involve ritual. But if ritual is a more tightly drawn category than mediation, Douglas has only shown that some mediations are rituals, though believing she has shown they all are.

Achievement In Context

Before Douglas, Durkheim argued that thought processes only had social origins in pre-modern societies, while in modern Western societies, knowledge could become truly objective. In *Purity and Danger*, Douglas shatters this view, demonstrating that all forms of knowledge can be set in their proper social context. It is an interesting direction, perhaps, for a lifelong Catholic (if all knowledge is socially contextual, where is the role for absolute truth?), but it may reflect the important role of institutions in shaping Douglas's own ideas, from her convent school to the Oxford Institute of Social Anthropology to the intellectual tradition of Durkheim.

As an example of the importance of context, Douglas shows us that an object is not out of place because it is dirty, but that it is dirty *because* it is out of place. "Shoes are not dirty in themselves, but it is dirty to place them on the dining-room table; food is not dirty in itself, but it is dirty to leave cooking utensils in the bedroom," she says.[1] Not for the first time, she is following Durkheim here, who in *The Division of Labor in Society* (his doctoral thesis) writes, "We must not say that an action shocks the common conscience because it is criminal, but rather that it is criminal because it shocks the common conscience."[2]

When Mary Douglas wrote *Purity and Danger* in 1966, it was a critical moment in the field of anthropology. The young field had grown up as a handmaiden of empire in both Britain and France. (Douglas's wartime service in the Colonial Office largely involved funding social anthropologists to explain to colonial officials the people they governed; or in her particular case, telling them funding would not return until after the war.) As decolonization and the disintegration of European empires gathered great speed in the mid-1960s, anthropology was in need of reinventing itself for a postcolonial* world. Instead of explaining the ways of the colonized to their colonizers, the new purpose, Douglas shows, can be showing us what we have in common.

Limitations

One limitation in *Purity and Danger* is Douglas's understanding of the world as not only rigidly structured, but also fairly static: A dirty object is "matter out of place," but it is not animated or particularly able to spread.[3] Pollution rules are mechanisms to protect the society in its overall shape, an ordered form that is contrasted with a surrounding yawning chasm of dangerous formlessness. But how can societies use ideas of pollution and purity to adapt to new situations, respond to fresh challenges, and evolve? Or are they by necessity conservative? And what if dirt is cyclically or simultaneously destructive and creative? What about forms of urbanization involved in the production of the city, such as when post-industrial "dirty" urban areas become sites of artistic generation? Can Douglas's paradigm help us to understand these, or is not suited for them?

Economist Joseph Schumpeter's* concept of creative destruction* also seems to involve "dirt" as the raw material of a subsequent stage of creative production, but Douglas's more static approach does not appear able to describe situations where dirt induces change rather than things staying the way they are.

Another possible limitation in Douglas's thought may be methodological. She tells us that ideas of bodily pollution, for tribes like the Coorg* of South India, express anxiety about bodily margins to reflect, and symbolically address, dangers to group survival. But ingenious as this is, how does she know this? Like many of her assertions, it is supported by neither evidence nor by argument, but expressed as self-evident. For someone who set out to make anthropology into a science, this seems possibly a strong failing indeed. "The place of this book in anthropology is like the invention of the frameless chassis in the history of car-design," she said ambitiously at the beginning of the book.[4]

NOTES

1   Mary Douglas, *Purity and Danger: An Analysis of Concepts of Pollution and Taboo*, vol. 2 of *Mary Douglas: Collected Works* (Abingdon: Routledge, 2002), 48.

2   Émile Durkheim, *The Division of Labor in Society,* trans. W. D. Halls (New York: Free Press, 1997), 81.

3   Douglas, *Purity and Danger*, 35.

4   Douglas, *Purity and Danger*, vii.

MODULE 8
PLACE IN THE AUTHOR'S WORK

KEY POINTS

- Mary Douglas maintained a lifelong interest in how institutional organization relates to patterns of belief, morality, and knowledge. She applied the ideas in *Purity and Danger* to understanding the belief systems of environmentalism and al-Qaeda.*

- Douglas pursued further scholarship on the Biblical books of Numbers and Leviticus, examining them in their literary structure. Numbers, she argued, was a ring-shaped work, while Leviticus was based on the floor plan of the ancient Israelite Tabernacle.*

- Douglas only returned to the Congo in 1987, where she discovered the Lele had largely been converted to Christianity, and practitioners of the beliefs she had documented in *Purity and Danger* were now persecuted for witchcraft.

Positioning

Purity and Danger: An Analysis of Concepts of Pollution and Taboo is Mary Douglas's most widely read and most influential work. Though its focus is on "dirt" and group identity, it set her on a path of exploring different aspects of social structure and belief in her subsequent successful career as a scholar.

Douglas is also well known for her 1970 book *Natural Symbols*, in which she argues that all institutions can be mapped in two dimensions: as high or low "grid" (defining and differentiating behaviors and rules) and by how strong their sense of "group" is (bonding with each other

> ❝ Our ideas of dirt also express symbolic systems …
> [The] difference between pollution behavior in one part
> of the world and another is only a matter of detail. ❞
>
> Mary Douglas, *Purity and Danger*

and dividing the world into insiders and outsiders). This hypothesis has inspired scholars to apply it to understanding corporations and policies from immigration to climate change, while also questioning how much our own capacity for rational argument is independent of the organizations to which we belong.

The key themes in *Purity and Danger*—how institutional organization relates to patterns of belief, morality, and understanding the world—continued to be the predominant themes of Douglas's lifelong research, along with understanding how groups define themselves as distinct from other groups.

Other areas in which Douglas subsequently applied the ideas in *Purity and Danger* include a 1982 book with Aaron Wildavsky, *Risk and Culture*, in which she compares modern environmentalism with religious beliefs of the past in terms of antipathy towards dominant power structures in society. Shortly before her death, she gave an interview in *The Spectator* magazine where she applied her cultural theory to discuss al-Qaeda and said the United States should allow the group to express its views, to draw them into society and dismantle "walls of virtue" its enclaves erected around themselves.

Douglas continues to explore these ideas in *The World of Goods*, and *Implicit Meanings: Essays in Anthropology*. In the second of these, she highlights how the lower social orders are also "those required to perform social functions equivalent to the excretory functions of the body"—there is a relationship between things we deem filthy and the people we demand clear them up.[1]

Integration

Douglas's fascination with the Old Testament, and in particular the Book of Leviticus, led her to focus further scholarship in that direction, learning Hebrew and refashioning her beliefs. She discarded her first interpretations of Jewish dietary laws and instead offered different, very creative interpretations of the same texts that were based more on their form than their content.

Douglas was also willing to evolve as a scholar while pursuing interests that remained constant. For example, she dismissed the main thesis of the third chapter of *Purity and Danger* in the preface to *Leviticus as Literature* (1999) and never mentioned again.

However, Douglas's fascination with larger intellectual structure remained. In *In the Wilderness*, her 1993 examination of defilement in the Book of Numbers, she argues that the Biblical text needs to be read as a ring-shaped poem. Her treatment of *Leviticus as Literature*, revealed only in the volume's denouement, is that Leviticus consists of three sections of text of unequal size, and its structure corresponds to the three chambers of the Israelite Tabernacle. Narrative sections on the consequences of breaking rules are placed, on the visual analogy, where screens divided the outermost, middle, and innermost chambers. Viewed within her life's work, this shows a willingness to begin again from scratch on her chosen subject, completely disregarding her most famous contribution to anthropology, *Purity and Danger's* application of the theory of pollution to the Bible.

By contrast, Douglas only returned to the Congo once, in 1987, to discover the Lele had largely become Christian, with beliefs such as the ones she had documented in *Purity and Danger* now persecuted as witchcraft.[2]

Significance

Much of the significance of Douglas's arguments in *Purity and Danger* can be viewed by looking at a small selection of the more than 20,000 works that cite it on the academic search engine Google Scholar. Academic work influenced by *Purity and Danger* spans texts such as (more predictably) Scottish anthropologist Victor Turner*'s 1969 *The Ritual Process: Structure and Anti-Structure,* in which he examines rituals of the Ndembu in Zambia, to (more surprisingly) American gender theorist Judith Butler's* 2011 *Bodies that Matter: On the Discursive Limits of Sex* and *Simians, Cyborgs, and Women* (2013).

Though Douglas always maintained that her theoretical contributions were independent of her Catholic upbringing and faith, the instinctive comfort she took in ritual, as well as hierarchical forms of social organization that after the 1960s became unfashionable, emerged not only in *Purity and Danger* but also in *Natural Symbols,* which presented a defense of now-deprecated customs such as fasting on Fridays. As an intellectual disciple of Durkheim, who was an atheist of a rabbinical Jewish background, she came to be regarded as a prominent Catholic intellectual.[3] Interestingly, her position in epistemology,* with its strong contextual element (where you sit determines where you stand), was often taken as if not relativism,* then quite near to it. Along with Clifford Geertz, she is regarded as one of the authors of classics of ethnography in the twentieth century. She is also regarded as a "New Durkheimian," due to her keen interest in institutions,[4] and was included in the 2007 book *Fifty Key Sociologists.*[5]

NOTES

1   Mary Douglas and Baron Isherwood, *World of Goods: Towards an Anthropology of Consumerism*, New York: Basic Books, 1979. Douglas, *Implicit Meanings: Essays in Anthropology*, London: Routledge & Kegan Paul, 1975, p. 155.

2   Mary Douglas, "Sorcery Accusations Unleashed: The Lele Revisited, 1987," *Africa: Journal of the International African Institute* 69, no. 2 (1999): 177.

3   See her inclusion in, e.g., J. L. Heft ed., *Believing Scholars: Ten Catholic Intellectuals* (New York: Fordham Univ. Press, 2005), 94–120.

4   6 Perri, ed., *The Institutional Dynamics of Culture: The New Durkheimians (Farnham, UK: Ashgate, 2008), 3.*

5   *J. Scott, ed., Fifty Key Sociologists: The Contemporary Theorists* (London: Routledge, 2007), 63–69.

SECTION 3
IMPACT

MODULE 9
THE FIRST RESPONSES

KEY POINTS

- Critics of Mary Douglas suggested that she did not attempt to explain why some traditional societies were not ridden with pollution concepts and wondered whether she underplayed hopes for the literal efficacy of rituals like rain dances.

- Douglas embraced the views of some of her readers, such as Ralph Bulmer's* critique that the question was not what the pangolin signified to members of the cult, but what social problems the cult was used to address.

- As a follower of Émile Durkheim, Douglas fell on a different side from Marxists* during the campus political wars of the 1960s. Her readership is strongest among religious students, political scientists, and neo-institutionalists.*

Criticism

While Mary Douglas's *Purity and Danger: An Analysis of Concepts of Pollution and Taboo* was quickly hailed as a significant and provocative book and was greeted with a largely admiring response, it also soon generated controversy.

In the book, Douglas attacks accepted wisdom and respected authors in her field robustly—so much so that Jack Dominian,* a psychiatrist and Catholic theologian, said her destructive criticism of previous works, especially James Frazer's *The Golden Bough*, "reads in places as the promised fulfilment of a personal vendetta."[1] Dominian also observed that Douglas at several points references Sigmund Freud, but suggested her arguments might have benefited from more

> ❝ Few anthropological texts can have had so notable an impact outside of that discipline. ❞
>
> Benjamin Campkin, "Placing 'Matter Out of Place': *Purity and Danger* as Evidence for Architecture and Urbanism"

engagement with other theorists in psychology, "such people as [Carl] Jung, [Alfred] Adler, the Neo-Freudians and the Behaviorists."[2]

Other readers questioned some of her broader methodological choices. P. H. Gulliver,* an anthropologist who had written about the Ndendeuli* of Tanzania, argued a large number of traditional societies are in fact not pollution-ridden, a fact that Douglas does not try to explain.[3] Finally, she may be correct in promulgating Durkheim's view of rituals as "making an emotional situation thinkable, and in making the mind accept pains which the body refuses to bear," but some readers wondered whether she had in fact overplayed slightly the immaterial efficacy of the symbolic activity as a motivation, as opposed to the hope—which Douglas was prepared to admit—that "rain rituals will cause rain, healing rituals avert death, harvest rituals produce crops."[4]

Responses

Purity and Danger attracted a larger audience to Douglas's earlier ethnographic research among the Lele. Accordingly, two anthropologist readers, Ralph Bulmer and Stanley Tambiah,* suggested that the question was not what the pangolin signified to members of the cult, but what social problems the cult was used to address. Bulmer, for example, had studied the cassowary in New Guinea, a bird that was used to symbolize the acute dilemmas around agricultural relations with in-laws. (In-law labor was needed in hoeing the highlands, but they could then establish their own claims to the land.) Tambiah had a similar account of the otter in northeast Thailand: "Anomalous" animals had ambiguous status in taxonomy precisely *because* they reflected social tensions and challenges. Douglas embraced their critique. She published their responses in a 1973 collection of readings, and in a 1972 Myers lecture adjusted her arguments to incorporate Bulmer's and Tambiah's evidence.

To her enormous credit, Douglas carefully considered the critiques of her treatment of the Old Testament dietary rules in *Purity and Danger* and amended her views in a series of three works published three decades later: *In the Wilderness: The Doctrine of Defilement in the Book of Numbers* (1993), *Leviticus as Literature* (1999), and *Jacob's Tears: The Priestly Work of Reconciliation* (2004). For this task, she went to the lengths of learning Hebrew and wrote a large number of academic articles, first trying out various arguments in Jewish Studies journals.[5]

Conflict And Consensus

Douglas's arguments explore the informal institutions of everyday social organization—not the state, or formal organizations—and treat culture as the dependent variable* (the thing to be explained), with social organization as the independent variable* (the thing to do the explaining).

In both of these respects, Douglas reflects the influence of Durkheim. As such, within the politicized campuses of the 1960s, she was on a different side of the debate than those who took their inspiration from Karl Marx. Marx, for example, took a low view of the division of labor (which he believed produces alienation), while Durkheim, a functionalist, believed the opposite: a division of labor created a feeling of solidarity between people. More broadly speaking, Marx emphasized conflict and turmoil and believed society is not a happy place; Durkheim and his disciples (and this includes Douglas) believed institutions jointly create a functional society, socializing its members into a consensus around values.

There is an emerging consensus that Douglas's view, expressed in *Purity and Danger* and subsequently, is correct: that impurity is a complex ritual structure, not a blunt instrument of social control and repression. In *Leviticus as Literature*, she calls the Jewish law something rather unique: a purity system that does not serve to subordinate castes or channel accusations.[6] It is telling that hardly any serious scholar has attempted to treat the taboos separately since her closely argued attempts at showing possible structures behind the individual prohibitions.

Douglas's contribution has also been pivotal in establishing new areas of consensus within the discipline of religious studies—in particular, her argument for the importance of not studying just religions, but instead "whole men and whole societies"[7] as they attempt to answer questions "about man's destiny and place in the universe."[8]

NOTES

1   Jack Dominian, "Purity and Danger (Review)," *New Blackfriars* 48, no. 557 (October 1966): 47.

2   Dominian, "Purity and Danger (Review)," 48.

3   P. H. Gulliver, "Purity and Danger (Review)," *Bulletin of the School of Oriental and African Studies* 30, no. 2 (1967): 462-464.

4   Mary Douglas, *Purity and Danger: An Analysis of Concepts of Pollution and Taboo*, vol. 2 of *Mary Douglas: Collected Works* (Abingdon: Routledge, 2002), 69 and 73.

5   These include "Atonement in Leviticus," *Jewish Studies Quarterly* 1.2 (1993/4): 109-130; "The Glorious Book of Numbers," *Jewish Studies Quarterly* 1.3 (1993/4): 193-216; and "The Stranger in the Bible," *Archives Européennes de Sociologie* 35.1 (1994): 283-298.

6   Mary Douglas, *Leviticus as Literature* (Oxford: Oxford University Press, 1999), VIII.

7   F.B. Welbourn, "Mary Douglas and the Study of Religion," *Journal of Religion in Africa* 3, no. 1 (1970): 89-95.

8   Douglas, *Purity and Danger*, 29.

MODULE 10
THE EVOLVING DEBATE

KEY POINTS

- Mary Douglas's argument has encouraged the development and widespread application of ideas of dirt and purity to understanding urban architecture, passages in the Bible other than the ones she analyzed, and regulation of environmental pollutants.

- Scholars have questioned some of her Old Testament examples, saying she misunderstood key words regarding animals that walk on their hands or swarm.

- Critics have generally neglected Douglas's nuanced arguments about the body and have applied her theory in its broadest-brush form.

Uses And Problems

As a result of her work in *Purity and Danger: An Analysis of Concepts of Pollution and Taboo*, Mary Douglas has a greater fame than any scholar working in her field. "When one reads essays and dissertations by students of psychology, medicine, social work, or psychotherapy, her name comes to light more than that of any other social anthropologist," said British anthropologist and psychiatrist Roland Littlewood.*[1] Her explanation of Jewish dietary laws in particular seized the imagination of non-anthropologists. Her ideas of dirt and classification are frequently referenced by people working in fields as far from her own as architecture, urban design, and sanitation.

A critical question that was eventually raised by readers of *Purity and Danger* regards her theory that anomaly underlies the kosher legislation found in Leviticus.

> **❝** Douglas's theory is utilized to imaginatively undermine tropes of order in iconic modernist architecture, and its material, constructional and aesthetic tenets. **❞**
>
> Benjamin Campkin, "Placing 'Matter Out of Place': *Purity and Danger* as Evidence for Architecture and Urbanism"

Edwin Firmage* and Walter Houston* reject Douglas's view that rejected ("dirty") animals within Judaism relate to proper locomotion in each sphere of the sky, land, and sea. While Douglas says "swarming things" are automatically excluded because they swarm, Firmage notes that the prohibited aquatic species in the Book of Leviticus 11.10 are a subset of "everything that swarms in the waters," and in Leviticus 11.21, the category of air-borne swarmers includes the clean species of locusts.[2]

Houston argues that swarming does not define a group according to mode of propulsion, and no equation is made between swarming in different spheres.[3] A related criticism is against Douglas's argument that the "swarming things" in Leviticus 11.29-30 are excluded for perversely walking upon their hands. According to Houston, this fails because the Hebrew term in question really refers to the palm of a hand or sole of a foot, and so in reality the text actually describes animals with padded feet (such as wolves, lions, and bears).

Schools Of Thought

It is worth placing *Purity and Danger* in context alongside other influential anthropological works also being written at the same time and after, especially around the question of deviance. For both Douglas and Durkheim, a shoe lying on a kitchen table or a morally shocking action should be understood relative to the society. If "there is no such thing as absolute dirt: it exists in the eye of the beholder," as Douglas says,[4] what about when the eye of the beholder changes? This is the step taken by Kai Erickson* in *Wayward Puritans*, an investigation into the community creation of deviance. For Erickson, deviance is more significant than Douglas's dirt as classificatory anomaly, with its ability to reboot society and create harmonious order; instead, deviance and conflict are fully needed by society in order to generate creative ideas that will challenge and strengthen it.

Douglas's research into purity in the case that so interested her—in the context of Leviticus and the preceding Book of Deuteronomy—was extended by a number of Old Testament scholars. One of these, Jacob Neusner,* a rabbi and religious studies scholar at Bard College, adapted Douglas's work on purity to look into how different sects of rabbis approached "clean" and "unclean" differently and how they linked literature about the Temple* to home life. (However, he ignored the model of the body, which lay at the core of Douglas's own thoughts on purity.)

A second Old Testament scholar, French philosopher Jean Soler,* in a 1979 study of the Genesis creation narrative, extended the application of Douglas's insights into cleanliness as wholeness and perfection to the creation story, the Temple system, and daily life. The Jesuit* scholar Jerome Neyrey* then applied Douglas's ideas of pollution and matter out of place to the role of Jesus in the Gospel of Mark,* who is perceived as "out of place" because he communed with unclean people (lepers, menstruants, and sinners), did not observe sacred classifications of space (the Temple) or time (the Sabbath*), and disregarded food rules and washing customs.

In Current Scholarship

Some scholarly arenas in which Douglas's work in *Purity and Danger* are applied are unsurprising: the regulation of environmental pollutants, violence and memory among Hutu refugees* in Tanzania, and power and deviance in Western society from 950 to 1250.

Other uses may surprise slightly: Architecture, urbanism, urban development, design, and sanitation all apparently have a particular affection for Douglas's theory, applying it in its broadest brushstrokes to evidence afforded by everyday things and spaces. The fascination with urban dirt—edgy, degraded neighborhoods at a city's core or in its periphery—has inspired the application of Douglas's theory as part of the development of "grunge aesthetics,"* "dirty realism,"* "junkspace,"* and the "urban pastoral."* The rejected, after all, is powerful and fascinating for Douglas. Obsessive surveillance of dirtier areas and the patrol of boundaries in an urban context have resonances with Douglas's work too, which has not escaped scholars working on these topics.

Literary and cultural studies also have applied Douglas's work, to explore the codification of dirt in texts as varied as those of Dante*, Jane Austen*, and Don DeLillo*. Meanwhile, art historians have used her work in the ambivalent role of dirt in art, alongside other frameworks like abjection.*

NOTES

1   Roland Littlewood, "Degrees of Mastery in the Work of Mary Douglas," *Anthropology Today* 14, no. 6 (December 1998): 1-2.

2   Edwin Firmage, "The Biblical Dietary Laws and the Concept of Holiness," in J.A. Emerton, *Studies in the Pentateuch* (Leiden: E.J. Brill, 1990), 185-6.

3   Walter Houston, *Purity and Monotheism: Clean and Unclean Animals in Biblical Law* (Sheffield: JSOT Press, 1993), 90-93.

4   Mary Douglas, *Purity and Danger: An Analysis of Concepts of Pollution and Taboo*, vol. 2 of *Mary Douglas: Collected Works* (Abingdon: Routledge, 2002), 12.

MODULE 11
IMPACT AND INFLUENCE TODAY

KEY POINTS

- Mary Douglas has had a vast impact both on academic research—there have been over 50,000 journal articles citing her—and broader public debate.

- Douglas's theory works in terms of binaries: things are clean, or dirty, but not normally in between. As a functionalist, her theory also is static and describes the workings of harmonious societies. This simplicity has helped her theory be very broadly applied, but also has attracted criticism.

- Douglas's academic discipline, anthropology, changed markedly during her career— partly as a result of her influence. At the start of her career, she was considered at the discipline's margins, but now she is considered one of the most important twentieth-century anthropologists.

Position

The influence of Mary Douglas's *Purity and Danger: An Analysis of Concepts of Pollution and Taboo*—not only on understanding questions of pollution and dirt, but also on the worlds of Old Testament scholarship and African anthropology—is so vast as to be virtually incalculable. She was the most frequently read British social anthropologist of her generation and a highly visible public intellectual whose work transcended academic boundaries.

Douglas wrote 19 books and taught generations of researchers and thinkers through her role as a leading professor at University College London, together with an 11-year career teaching at American universities including Princeton and Northwestern.

> ❝ Without doubt, 25 years of feminist work has enlarged understanding of gender issues beyond the insights of even such an original thinker as Mary Douglas. Nevertheless, many of the ideas which have sprouted since can be found in this slim, controversial and still highly relevant volume. ❞
>
> Leonore Davidoff, *Times Higher Education Supplement*

In the public eye, Douglas attracted attention by criticizing the Catholic Church's decision to abandon its practice of Friday abstinence from meat, saying rituals of that nature bound people together and created a sense of solidarity.

But it is *Purity and Danger* for which she is best known and which contains the kernels of all her theories and academic interests, which she spent the remainder of an extremely fruitful and visible career refining, exploring, and occasionally reinventing.

Purity and Danger is also a rich source of ideas and hypotheses, many not yet given adequate attention. Areas of her work that have been so far overlooked include exploring with greater nuance how the body relates, through ritual, to broader society and its challenges.

Douglas has influenced contemporary thinking on dirt and purity directly through her own writing and also indirectly, through scholarship provoked by her ideas. According to Google Scholar, there have been over 50,000 journal articles citing Mary Douglas.

Interaction

Perhaps precisely because Douglas's model of dirt and systems of classification is now one of the best-known and most broadly used tools in analyzing social reality today, critiques of it have only grown more widespread.

One persistent criticism has been that Douglas thinks in terms of binaries: for her, things are clean or dirty, but they are not in a midway state. This gives her theory strength in making it generate strong predictions and interpretations; at the same time, it means her theory may not be as well suited to deal with shades of difference and complexity. (Conversely, a defender of Douglas may say beginning from such strong distinctions follows directly from her claim that belief structures all involve systems of classification.) Another criticism has been that her thinking is static and prioritizes social harmony. This is good for a broadly well-functioning society, less so for those whose lives are beset by torment, tumultuous change, and class conflict. (This last criticism is particularly frequent from people in the Marxian* tradition.)

Social anthropology advanced quite substantially in Douglas's lifetime, and largely due to her influence. At the time of her emigration to the United States in 1977, she felt her position was rather peripheral within her field; but when she returned, she was showered with honors (including being made a dame, Britain's female equivalent of a knight) and was elected a Fellow of the British Academy in 1989.

She spent her later years refining her theoretical statements and delving deeper into the Old Testament texts, stung by and responding to earlier accusations that her exciting grand theory was erected on casual scholarship.

The Continuing Debate

Interesting insight into the current debate about the ideas in *Purity and Danger* can be gleaned from glancing at a few examples of more recent scholarship that takes her work as a starting point.

One group of researchers has found that a sensitivity to impurity corresponds to an increased likelihood of displaying conservative attitudes and voting patterns.[1] Meanwhile, a second set of authors, drawing on Douglas, has found that discourse around science often mixes language of purity alongside themes of objectivity and truth in scientific frames of reference, and the same mix often surfaces in representations and appeals by the state.[2]

Looking further back in history, a 2014 book called *Dirty Old London* applies Douglas's categories to chart how Victorian London and its administrators and reformers defined and managed categories of dirt, including waste (ash, mud, excrement, corpses), bodies (washing and excretion), buildings (slums), disease (cholera and typhus), and pollution (smoke, soot, miasma).[3]

In modern financial services, new forms of dirt—such as risks involving cybersecurity—must be regulated and, ideally, cleaned or otherwise managed, including through new forms of insurance. Michalis Lianos,* building on Douglas's work, has drawn attention to this process (which he calls "dangerization"*) as a way of conceiving of new future events in terms of danger and subjecting them to systems of automatic controls that will remove the danger and lead back to a normal state of safety. "This is a useful reminder that [Douglas] does not stand still," writes sociologist Ian Hacking.* [4]

NOTES

1   Yoel Inbar, David Pizarro, Ravi Iyer and Jonathan Haidt, "Disgust Sensitivity, Political Conservatism, and Voting," *Social Psychological and Personality Science* 3 (2012): 537.

2   Scott Clifford and Dane G. Wendell, "How Disgust Influences Health Purity Attitudes," *Political Behavior* 38, no. 1 (2016), 155-178.

3   Lee Jackson, *Dirty Old London: The Victorian Fight Against Filth* (New Haven: Yale University Press, 2014).

4   Ian Hacking, "Risk and Dirt," in Richard Ericson and Aaron Doyle, eds., *Risk and Morality* (Toronto: University of Toronto Press, 2003), 29.

MODULE 12
WHERE NEXT?

KEY POINTS

- Questions of dirt and pollution are even more relevant today, with rapid growth in developing countries and climate change only increasing the salience of dirt. Mary Douglas saw symbols as important routes to understanding classificatory systems, which in turn reflect and symbolize a social order.

- Part of the reason why Douglas's contributions remain so salient even today has to do with how she links social structure and society's needs with the symbolic realm of culture. Later scholarship often focused only on one or the other, whereas part of her great strength is showing how they are linked.

- Correctly understanding Douglas, her limitations, and arguments made by critics of her approach—and being able to recognize when her concepts are incorrectly understood or applied—is indispensable in the field of management, given how influential and widespread her ideas have become.

Future Directions

In *Purity and Danger: An Analysis of Concepts of Pollution and Taboo*, Mary Douglas takes readers on an important journey through the shift in anthropology from structure to process. If she revealed processes behind fairly settled systems of dirt management in stable societies such as the Lele and ancient Israel, then it remains for today's scholars to look into unsettled problems and situations of rapid change. How contemporary societies solve their problems of dirt, refuse, and pollution, who makes

> **"**On the one hand, Douglas' approach opens up architecture and urbanism to interdisciplinary thinking and bodies of contextual evidence that prioritize the cultural significance of the everyday and the excluded. However, Douglas' theory contains unresolved tensions between material and conceptual evidence, and between dirt as matter or symbol, and these are at the heart of dirt as a research trope. **"**
>
> Benjamin Campkin, "Placing 'Matter Out of Place': *Purity and Danger* as Evidence for Architecture and Urbanism"

these decisions, and how they are disputed, both in the developed and the developing world, is now not just an academic matter.

China, with its rapid growth and industrialization, now produces fully one third of the world's waste and by 2030 will produce three times more waste than the United States.[1] (It also, until 2017, purchased waste from the US and other developed countries; India continues to do so.[2]) We also have to grapple with dirt in the air: Emissions from coal and gas production grew by more than 65 percent from 2000 to 2016.[3] And with cattle belch responsible for fully a quarter of global methane emissions, what may not for previous generations have been dirt (but, in contrast to the dirt of cities, an idyll of rural clean living) is now an important source of pollution to be managed.[4]

Dirt is increasingly relevant for the future—and so will be conversations about how to manage it. One example is the emerging interdisciplinary field of discard studies, which questions what seems normal in what we discard, and examines practices and relationships around the act of discarding. A second is the environmental humanities, which looks to linkages between the sciences and humanities in creating more unified ways of knowing the natural world, and the place of humans in it.

Potential

One of Douglas's achievements in *Purity and Danger* is introducing into the English-language tradition of research Émile Durkheim's insight that rituals offer important material for understanding a society's central values and tensions in an intensely concentrated form. This is true whether the subject at hand is ancient Israel, sub-Saharan Africa, or new emerging rituals of modern life in the urban West dealing with questions framed in terms of purity and pollution in immigration, the internet, the climate, radicalization, or public health.

Another related achievement of *Purity and Danger* is its quite unusual mixture of research in anthropology and sociology with perspectives from as broad a range of fields as religious studies, cognitive sciences, and the arts.

Douglas, drawing on Durkheim, links symbols with social institutions and sees symbols as routes to understanding classificatory systems that, in turn, reflect and symbolize a social order. Compare her symbol-centered approach to actor-centered perspectives like those espoused by Fredrik Barth* in the transactionalist* tradition: While he might see a maverick as a possible entrepreneur, disrupter, and bringer of needed change, Mary Douglas would view him foremost as a classificatory anomaly and then look into both the danger and power of that role. The tradition of symbolic anthropology that Douglas did so much to create raced forward with Clifford Geertz's equally interdisciplinary work in Java* and David Schneider's* work in the Micronesian island of Yap.* Geertz's "thick description,"* highly influential to social scientists working at the moment, takes much inspiration from Douglas in *Purity and Danger*.

One explanation for the durability of Douglas's work is how it links the symbolic realm of culture, taken seriously in its own right, with social structure and its needs. As anthropology became a more specialized field from the 1990s onward, these two elements were increasingly studied independently of each other. Douglas offers a compelling example of how the two can be usefully intertwined in a way that offers a deeper understanding and in which each contributes to greater understanding of the other.

Summary
In the preface to a 2002 edition of *Purity and Danger*, Douglas says the idea of writing a treatise on dirt and contagion came together in her head when she had caught "one of the contagious diseases, measles, I think," and was laid up in bed for a week.[5]

She said she was "stunned with surprise" when Routledge gave her a contract with a £100 advance and feared, from its slow sales in the first two years after its publication, that her book was a flop.[6] It turns out it was not. In fact, people who work in the field say *Purity and Danger* is both an "academic bestseller" and a bridge between the British and French traditions of looking at society.[7]

Man creates the holy, says Douglas, by putting it in its place. Thus she reconciles one of the great puzzles: how to fit together the concepts of pollution and defilement with holiness. The universality of pollution beliefs, symbolically drawing lines around the sacred, creates and preserves the boundaries by which social and moral order can exist. This is no less the case for contemporary urban, Western societies than for traditional or ancient ones: All of them create order, using ritual to diminish ambiguity and indiscretion.

While it is important to understand and be able to apply the powerful tools and concepts Douglas outlines in *Purity and Danger*, it is equally important to understand their limitations and criticisms—and to recognize when they are being used incorrectly. The tools from *Purity and Danger* and the information in this analysis now put budding sociologists, anthropologists, and religious scholars in a position to begin doing this.

NOTES

1   Gwynn Guilford, "China's Mountains of Garbage," *The Atlantic*, March 25, 2013, accessed December 3, 2017, https://www.theatlantic.com/china/archive/2013/03/chinas-mountains-of-garbage/274329/.

2   Pak Yiu, "China Ban on Waste Imports Leads to Piles of Paper Abroad, Surging Prices in China," Reuters, September 28, 2017, accessed January 20, 2017, https://www.reuters.com/article/us-china-hongkong-paperrecycling/china-ban-on-waste-imports-leads-to-piles-of-paper-abroad-surging-prices-in-china-idUSKCN1C30GR.

3   Damian Carrington, "Global Carbon Emissions Stood Still in 2016, Offering Climate Hope," *Guardian*, September 28, 2017, accessed December 3, 2017, https://www.theguardian.com/environment/2017/sep/28/global-carbon-emissions-stood-still-in-2016-offering-climate-hope.

4   Carrington, "Global Carbon Emissions."

5   Mary Douglas, *Purity and Danger: An Analysis of Concepts of Pollution and Taboo*, vol. 2 of *Mary Douglas: Collected Works* (Abingdon: Routledge, 2002), x.

6   Douglas, *Purity and Danger*, x.

7   Thomas Hyllan Eriksen and Finn Sivert Nielsen, *A History of Anthropology* (London: Pluto Press, 2013), 124.

GLOSSARY

GLOSSARY OF TERMS

Abjection: casting away part of a person's identity. An example of abjection used in psychoanalysis is that we separate ourselves from our mothers, then use rituals to maintain clear boundaries against what is maternal.

al-Qaeda: a militant Islamist organization founded by Osama bin Laden and other associates in 1988. It is responsible for several terrorist attacks directed against the United States. After the death of bin Laden in 2011, the group has been led by Egyptian Ayman al-Zawahiri.

Anomy (or **anomie**): the breakdown of social bonds between an individual and the community. Émile Durkheim* used the term in his 1897 book *Suicide*, where he diagnoses anomy as a symptom of a breakdown of organic solidarity* successfully binding an individual into a society.

Anthropology: the scientific study of human beings and culture. Formal learned societies devoted to anthropology first appeared in Paris in 1859 and London in 1863. Social anthropology,* with an emphasis on participant observation and cross-cultural comparison, developed in the early twentieth century.

Anthropological modernism: the dominant movement in anthropology in Britain between the 1920s and 1980, championing the value of intensive fieldwork and participant observation, with a theoretical emphasis on how social practices fit together to create a coherent social system.

Armchair anthropologist: dismissive term for early anthropologists of the nineteenth century who relied on missionaries and colonial officials to collect and record data from the field, with the work of the scholar chiefly taking the form of integrating evidence and constructing theory.

Baby boomers: the generational cohort born between the mid-1940s and early 1960s. In both North America and Europe, this generation benefited from increasing affluence and subsidized higher education and is associated with rejection or redefinition of earlier traditional values.

Bashilele: another name for the Lele* people.

Behaviorist: in psychology and philosophy, those who focus on understanding the behavior of humans and other animals in terms of stimuli and responses. Behaviorism arose in the 1910s, and led to a counter-movement in the 1960s, the "cognitive revolution," which looked at internal processes such as consciousness and inward experience.

Book of Leviticus: the third book of both the Torah (the first five books of the Bible outlining Jewish* law) and Old Testament.* The title comes from the Greek word Leviticus (Λευιτικόν), which literally renders the Hebrew phrase "law of priests." Much of the book concerns priestly offerings relating to the Tabernacle, which housed the Ark of the Covenant.

Book of Numbers: the fourth book of the Bible, which treats of the return of the Israelites from Egypt before they had taken possession of the land of Canaan.

British Empire: dominions, colonies, and other territories administered by the United Kingdom (and before 1800, the Kingdom of Great Britain). At its height, it was the largest empire in history, covering nearly a quarter of the Earth's land area.

Catharsis: the purging and purification of emotions, especially pity and fear, through art or ritual. Aristotle describes it as being one of the characteristics of tragedy in the *Poetics*.

Catholic: a Christian* belonging to the Roman Catholic Church, which is under the leadership of the Pope, as Bishop of Rome, and ultimately administered from the Holy See, with its geographical base in Vatican City. Roughly half of Christians are Catholic.

Christian: a follower of Christianity, the religion based on the life and teachings of Jesus of Nazareth.*

Colonialism: the process of mainly European settlement over other areas of the world, including the Americas, Africa, and Asia. Following the exhaustion of the main colonial powers, chiefly Britain and France, after World War II,* colonized territories largely gained their independence in a process which began with India and Pakistan in 1947 and gained its greatest momentum in the 1960s.

Congo Crisis: a period of upheaval between 1960 and 1965 in today's Democratic Republic of the Congo, then the Republic of the Congo. It followed the departure of colonial rule from Belgium in 1960 and was aggravated by the Cold War, with both the United States and Soviet Union supporting opposing factions.

Continent: a shorthand expression for the European Continent, the countries of Europe excluding the United Kingdom and Ireland (and generally Iceland as well).

Coorg: a former state in southern India also frequently known as Kodagu, which in 1956 was merged with the state of Mysore (now called Karnataka).

Creative destruction: a term used by Joseph Schumpeter* to describe the force of the capitalist* market in continually destroying long-standing arrangements through new technology. Rather than market processes resulting in an equilibrium, Schumpeter saw a process by which short-lived equilibria were constantly replaced.

Crucifixion: a method of capital punishment in which a victim is nailed or tied to a large wooden beam and left to die over several days from a combination of exhaustion and asphyxiation. In ancient Rome, it was reserved for slaves, pirates, and enemies of the state. The Crucifixion of Jesus of Nazareth* took place between 30 and 33 A.D.

Cultural anthropology: a branch of anthropology* that focuses on the study of cultural variation among individual humans. It dominates anthropology in the United States. In the rest of the world, social anthropology,* which seeks to explain symbols, rituals, and narratives of societies, is dominant.

Dangerization: a tendency to perceive and analyze the world through categories of menace. In an article in 2000, Mary Douglas and Michalis Lianos said that after Émile Durkheim* and Michel Foucault,* the idea of deviance from a community's norms has been the central principle for explaining crime and justifying punishment, and that dangerization was a response to anomie* in reinforcing social norms.

Decolonization: the process following the predominant breakup of the British Empire* and the transition of formerly colonized territories to independence. Formerly colonized countries played a large role in the Non-Aligned Movement during the Cold War, where previously colonized countries declined to ally either with the United States and its allies or the Communist Bloc.

Dependent variable: in social science research, the variable which a hypothesis under investigation is attempting to explain.

Dirty realism: a literary style investigating the seamier or more mundane aspects of modern life, coined in a summer 1983 edition of the literary magazine *Granta*.

Durkheimian: an adjective used to describe the school, an approach, or the group of subsequent scholars highly influenced by the work of French positivist sociologist Émile Durkheim.* Durkheimian approaches include seeking the roots of social behavior in religion or examining levels of social integration and control between societies.

Edwardian: the period in British history and that of the British Empire from 1901 to 1910, following the Victorian* era and marked by the rule of King Edward VII in the United Kingdom.

Empiricist: a proponent of the viewpoint within epistemology* that knowledge comes only or chiefly from sensory experience, including scientific experimentation.

Enlightenment: an eighteenth-century intellectual movement that was closely associated with the Scientific Revolution, together with the spread of ideas of individual liberty and religious tolerance and opposition to absolutist rule and questioning of religious orthodoxy. Key early Enlightenment thinkers included René Descartes, Jean-Jacque Rousseau, and Voltaire in France; John Locke in England;

David Hume and Adam Smith in Scotland; and Immanuel Kant in Germany.

Epistemology: the branch of philosophy concerned with understanding knowledge. Key questions within it include what constitutes justified grounds for belief and the scope and limits of truth, belief, and justification.

Ethnographic: relating to the systematic study of people and cultures, generally gained through participant observation or extensive interview, and presenting a holistic study recording all observed behavior and describing all relationships between symbols and meanings. It is a key component of anthropology* as well as sociology and other social sciences.

Gerontocracy: rule by the aged, in which the oldest members of society either hold formal leadership positions or otherwise dominate these positions.

***Gestalt* school:** an approach, often opposed to structural functionalism,* that sees the mind as imposing meaningful structures on a chaotic world. The *gestalt* in question is a form or shape, referencing the principle that humans naturally perceive the world in terms of organized patterns and objects.

Gospel of Mark: the second book of the New Testament, which begins with the baptism of Jesus of Nazareth* (it does not include a birth narrative) and concludes with the discovery of the empty tomb (similarly, it does not include post-Resurrection appearances). As such, it is the shortest and presumed earliest (roughly A.D. 66-70) of the four Gospels.

Grunge aesthetics: a sense of taste associated with a subculture of grunge music appearing in the mid-1980s in the American Pacific Northwest, in cities such as Seattle, fusing elements of punk rock with heavy metal. Grunge as a movement may be considered to have ended with the suicide of Nirvana's Kurt Cobain in 1994. However, as an influence on fashion, it reappeared thereafter on the runway, including in the work of Yves Saint Laurent's Hedi Slimane in 2008 and 2013. If punk was considered anti-fashion, grunge was un-fashion, associated with realism, streetwear, and non-conformism.

Heterotopias: within Michel Foucault's* human geography, places and spaces that involve concentration of the other, such as boarding schools (separating those coming of age from the rest of society), prisons or asylums (separating those whose behavior is outside the norm), or time (museums, enclosing objects from different times).

Hierophanies: a manifestation of the sacred, especially for the religious historian Mircea Eliade,* who sees hierophanies as the foundation of religion and as the breaking through of the sacred into the profane world.

Hutu refugees: displaced people of a Bantu ethnic group primarily living in Rwanda, Burundi, and the eastern Democratic Republic of the Congo. In April 1994, an estimated two million Rwandans fled to neighboring countries following the country's genocide; most of them were Hutu.

Independent variable: in experimental research, the cause or causes, sometimes referred to as an explanatory variable(s), which are hypothesized to affect another, dependent variable.*

Israelite Tabernacle: according to the Old Testament,* the dwelling place of God during the time the ancient Jews* had left Egypt and before they had established themselves in Canaan. It is principally described in the Old Testament Book of Exodus.

Israelites: a confederation of tribes of the ancient Near East who feature in the Old Testament* and from whom modern Jews* are descended.

Java: an island of Indonesia, home to more than half of Indonesia's population and including the nation's capital city of Jakarta.

Jesuits: formally known as the Society of Jesus, a scholarly organization of Catholic* priests and brothers founded by St. Ignatius of Loyola, originating in sixteenth-century Spain and with 16,378 members in 2017.

Jews: ethnic and religious group originating from the Israelites of Middle Eastern antiquity whose traditional religion is Judaism.*

Judaism: an ancient religion with a 3,000-year history, originating in the Middle East and based upon the books of the Jewish Bible (or Old Testament*).

Judea: a name used in antiquity and in the Old Testament to describe the contemporary mountainous southern portion of Israel and the West Bank. The territory was governed as the Roman province of Judea (or Iudaea) between the years A.D. 6 and 135.

Junkspace: a concept created by Rotterdam-based architecture theorist Rem Koolhas which describes modern spatial organization, from the shopping mall and airport to the convention center and

hotel, as seamless, provisional, and unlinked to the past. In his 2001
essay "Junkspace," Koolhas describes junkspace as "orphaned" and
"authorless, yet surprisingly authoritarian."

Kalahari Desert: a 900,000-square-kilometer, semi-arid savanna in
southern Africa that covers much of Botswana as well as parts of
Namibia and South Africa.

Kashrut: a set of Jewish religious dietary laws prescribing what is
kosher, or fit for consumption. Most of its basic laws are set down in
the Books of Leviticus* and Deuteronomy.

!Kung: a San people living in the Kalahari Desert* which spans
Namibia, Botswana, and South Africa. Historically living in semi-
permanent camps of ten to thirty individuals based around bodies of
water, their language is known for its extensive use of click consonants
such as the tenuis (post)alveolar click represented by the symbol !.

Lele: an African tribe studied by Mary Douglas. A subgroup of the
Kuba people who live in the Democratic Republic of Congo, many
have migrated to the country's capital, Kinshasa, since she conducted
her research, and evangelical activity has converted many of them to
Christianity* from traditional religions.

Marxian: a school of economic thought that makes use of concepts
initially identified by Karl Marx* and his collaborator Friedrich
Engels, which might include elements of crisis in capitalism, processes
of economic evolution, and the origin of economic value. Economic
work on the business cycle, as well as Joseph Schumpeter's* ideas of
creative destruction,* draw on the Marxian approach that market
economies change over time, rather than reaching a single stable
equilibrium.

Marxist: generally speaking, a person or approach quite close to the normative ideas of classical Marxism, which include giving primacy to economic analysis in explaining social change, as well as the application to politics of Karl Marx's concepts of class consciousness, alienation, and exploitation as developed in the three volumes of *Das Kapital.* Marxist also more often references a political orientation, where Marxian more broadly indicates any school of economic thought drawing on Marx's concepts.

Mechanical solidarity: for Émile Durkheim,* mechanical solidarity occurs in traditional and small-scale societies, where cohesion arises because of the homogeneity of individuals, through a commonality of lifestyle, educational or religious training, or relationship through kinship networks.

Medical materialism: a term introduced by William James* in *Varieties of Religious Experience* to describe the explanation of states of mind by physical causes. He suggests as an example explaining the conversion of Paul/Saul of Tarsus on the road to Damascus by reference to epilepsy, or love by the action of hormones. For James, the mental states in question may have validity in their own right, while also corresponding to accompanying physical states: Thus Paul may have both experienced a light from heaven, and an epileptic seizure.

Modern societies: societies that have been through industrialization (and in some cases are now post-industrial), whose orientation has shifted comparatively speaking more to the future than to the past, and which are characterized by a strong nation-state, mass democracy, and a market economy.

Ndendeule or **Ndendeuli:** an ethnic and linguistic group inhabiting the Ruvuma region of southern Tanzania. In her 1970 book *Natural*

Symbols, Mary Douglas characterizes the Ndendeule as egalitarian, with no chiefs and no person remaining in a position of eminence over others over a long term.

Neo-Freudians: a group of loosely linked, chiefly American theorists influenced by Sigmund Freud,* many of whom attempted to restate Freudian theory in terms of sociology.*

Neo-Institutionalist: one who explores through sociology the roles of institutions, including by borrowing methods from economics to study political institutions, responding to and largely replacing the previous scholarly movement of behavioralism.

New Testament: in the Christian* Bible, the collection of four Gospels, Acts of the Apostles, Epistles, and Book of Revelation, generally coming to 27 books and centered around the life and death of Jesus of Nazareth* and the subsequent early Christian church.

Nuer: an ethnic group living mainly in South Sudan, and partly in southwestern Ethiopia. The Nuer historically live a semi-nomadic, pastoralist lifestyle, herding cattle for survival.

Old Testament: the Jewish* Bible, which forms the first portion also of the Christian* Bible. In the Jewish text (of which the traditional Hebrew text is known as the Masoretic Text, and often referred to as the Tanakh), there are 24 books. The number of books in the Christian canons is slightly larger, partly due to the division of several books (Samuel, Chronicles, and Ezra-Nehemiah among them). Scholars believe the first five books (called the Pentateuch in Christianity, and Torah in Judaism*) reached their present form by around 400 B.C., the Prophetic books between 140 and 116 B.C., and the remaining books (called "Writings" in Judaism) thereafter.

Organic solidarity: for Émile Durkheim* in *The Division of Labour in Society* (1893), organic solidarity refers to the mutual dependence individuals have on one another in modern and industrial societies. Thus, farmers produce the food that allows factory workers to produce tractors in turn to enable them to more efficiently produce food.

Pangolin: a nocturnal mammal species whose members live in hollow trees or burrows and use an acute sense of smell to find and consume insects. Native to Africa and Asia, pangolins have extremely long tongues as well as protective keratin scales covering their skin.

Postcolonial: a term used either to refer to societies previously subject to colonial rule, or the academic study of legacies of colonial control (a field known as postcolonial studies).

Post-Enlightenment societies: a term to describe societies, largely in Western Europe and North America, which experienced spread in the eighteenth and nineteenth centuries of Enlightenment ideas of reason and progress, and today have public discourses dominated by assumptions of liberalism, science, and secularism.

Postmodern turn: a term used to describe the departure from modernism in the middle to late twentieth century across a variety of disciplines, sharing an attitude of skepticism, rejection of grand or universalized narratives, and instead prioritizing individual experience, processes of social construction, relativism, and plural truths. Key thinkers in this turn include Jacques Derrida and Jean-François Lyotard.

Relativism: a view holding that each point of view has its own truth, which is always particular to a frame of reference. Relativism would hold that beliefs and behaviors need to be understood within local contexts, rather than as universal truths.

Rosary: a form of prayer used particularly in the Catholic* church, consisting of a string of knots or beads used for purposes of counting prayers. The word derives from Latin *rosarium*, meaning a garland of roses. As a devotion, it became popular in the twelfth century.

Ruminants: mammals that chew their cud. These species acquire nutrients from plant-based food by fermenting it in a specialized stomach with the assistance of microbes, a process typically requiring the fermented ingesta (cud) to be regurgitated and chewed further prior to digestion.

Sabbath: a day within Judaism* and Christianity* set aside for abstention from work and devoted to the performance of religious duties. Within Judaism, it is celebrated from sunset on Friday until sunset on Saturday; in Christianity, on Sunday.

Sacred contagion: a belief that spiritual properties corresponding to a person, place, or object may be passed along to another. Émile Durkheim* identifies the term in his book *The Elementary Forms of Religious Life*, whereas Mary Douglas distinguishes cultures where concepts of sacred contagion are commonplace from others where they are not.

Social anthropology: the dominant branch of anthropology* in the United Kingdom, Commonwealth countries, and France, which attempts to explain narratives, rituals, and symbolic behavior by their social context, as opposed to cultural anthropology,* which focuses on explaining cultural variation between societies.

Social geographers: Scientists who study people and their environment, with a particular emphasis on social factors as well as spatial ones (having to do with location).

Social structures: patterned social arrangements that both emerge from, and partially determine, the acts of individuals. These include institutions, the class structure, and other patterned relations within large social groups.

Sociology: an academic discipline devoted to scientific study of societies, their development, structure, and function, largely beginning with the work of Émile Durkheim.*

Structural functionalism: an approach in scholarship that sees society as a complex system with parts that work together to promote solidarity and stability. According to sociologist Anthony Giddens, this approach looks to biology as the model for social science. Prominent practitioners of structural-functionalist approaches include Talcott Parsons, Auguste Comte, and Herbert Spencer.

Student movements: a series of social protests peaking in the 1960s civil rights movement and anti-Vietnam War activism in the United States, while the May 1968 protests in France saw students join widespread worker agitation, and West German student activists accused the Bundesrepublik (the Federal Republic of Germany) of authoritarianism and hypocrisy, particularly with reference to the wartime pasts of government and university officials.

Taboo: prohibited actions based on behavior either seen as accursed or sacred. British explorer Captain James Cook introduced the term to English from Tongan in 1777, when it was explained to him certain things were "consecrated, inviolable, forbidden, unclean, or cursed."

Sigmund Freud* afterward characterized incest and patricide as universal taboos. Franz Steiner,* in a series of lectures brought out posthumously in 1956, argued that the notion of taboo is as common to Western societies as ancient and traditional ones.

Temple: the Second Temple constructed on the Temple Mount in Jerusalem as a religious center for Judaism* was erected in 516 BCE and lasted until the year 70. As the symbolic and ceremonial fulcrum of Jewish life, it took the place of Solomon's Temple which had stood on the site until destroyed in 587 BCE.

Thick description: in ethnography* and other social sciences, a way of presenting an individual or group's behavior while offering sufficient context to make that behavior intelligible to an outside observer.

Traditional society: a pre-industrial society, one that Émile Durkheim* would describe as bound together by mechanical rather than organic solidarity.*

Transactionalist: proponents of transactionalism, an approach articulated by John Dewey and Fredrik Barth* that sees individuals as embedded and integrated in a world of exchange and rejects ideas of absolute knowledge and ultimate truth in favor of seeing identity and knowledge as arising out of these constant interactions with others.

Urban pastoral: a literary style that explores items of urban architecture, such as skyscrapers, concrete, and underground transport, in a celebratory mode similar to how earlier Romantic writers described the rural countryside. It is especially associated with a group of poets referred to as the New York School, including Frank O'Hara, John Ashbery, and Barbara Guest.

Usilele: another name for the Lele* people.

Victorian period: the period from 1837 to 1901, corresponding to the reign of Queen Victoria in the British Empire, a time characterized by comparative peace, political liberalization, and industrialization.

World War I: also known as the Great War or First World War, a global war originating in Europe lasting from July 1914 to November 1918 and pitting the British Empire, Russian Empire, and French Third Republic, eventually joined by the United States, against the central European powers of Germany and Austria-Hungary. Over 18 million combatants and civilians died in the course of the war, which saw new technology and industrial capacity applied in the war effort and a protracted period of stalemated trench warfare.

World War II: a global war lasting from 1939 to 1945, marked by over 50 million deaths. Direct consequences included the end of European colonial rule, the start of the Cold War, and political and economic integration within Europe.

Yap: an island located in the Caroline Islands of the western Pacific and politically part of the Federated States of Micronesia.

PEOPLE MENTIONED IN THE TEXT

Alfred Adler (1870-1937) was an Austrian medical doctor, psychotherapist, and founder of the school of individual psychology, who researched feelings of inferiority and the social role in individual adjustment.

Dante Alighieri (c. 1265-1321) was an Italian poet of the late Middle Ages and early Renaissance, whose *Divine Comedy* was one of the most important poems of the period, as well one of the most important in the history of the Italian language.

Jane Austen (1775-1817) was an English novelist whose six major novels, which are known for their realism and irony, critique and comment on the lives of the British landed gentry of the late 18th century.

Fredrik Barth (1928-2016) was a Norwegian social anthropologist.* He is best known for his concept of transactionalism,* which looks at society in terms of human exchange and emphasizes the integration of individuals within society through these constant processes of exchange.

Zygmunt Bauman (1925-2017) was a Polish sociologist and philosopher who after 1971 lived in the United Kingdom, where he was Professor of Sociology at the University of Leeds. among other topics, Bauman wrote about the ambivalence modern consumer-oriented societies take toward the strange and unfamiliar: it is enticing, as with new fashions in food or dress, but also the object of fear, as it cannot be controlled or classified.

Ralph Bulmer (1928-1988) was an ethnobiologist and social anthropologist* at the University of Auckland. He documented the way the Kalam people of New Guinea interacted with birds, particularly the cassowary, a flightless bird living in the rain forest.

Judith Butler (b. 1956) is an American philosopher and gender theorist. Much of her work develops a view of gender as a theatrical performance with a set of scripts handed down across time.

James Clifford (b. 1945) was for 30 years a professor in the History of Consciousness Department at the University of California, Santa Cruz, until retiring in 2011. He contributed important critiques of ethnography* during anthropology's* process of post-colonial self-criticism in the 1980s.

Don DeLillo (b. 1936) is an American novelist, playwright, and essayist, whose work explores the dehumanizing aspects of modern American life.

Jack Dominian (1929-2014) was a British psychiatrist and Roman Catholic* theologian. He was particularly influential for his studies of marital breakdown.

Émile Durkheim (1858-1917) was a French sociologist, often considered one of the founders of modern social science. He was particularly interested in how norms, beliefs, and collective consciousness create and sustain societies, based on fundamentally egoistical individuals.

Mircea Eliade (1907-1986) was a Romanian scholar of religion at the University of Chicago. His division of experience into sacred and profane using the concept of hierophanies* (breakthroughs of the sacred into daily life) has remained influential to the present day; for him, those partaking in rituals take part in, and do not merely commemorate, hierophanies in their own minds.

Kai Erickson (b. 1931) is an American sociologist whose early work looked at the late seventeenth-century Salem witch trials and frameworks for understanding normality and deviance. His later work investigated social consequences of catastrophic events.

Sir E. E. Evans-Pritchard (1902-1973) was a professor of social anthropology* at the University of Oxford from 1946 to 1970. His early research was on the Nuer* people of the upper Nile, and he was instrumental in the early development of social anthropology* in Britain.

Edwin Firmage is a scholar of the Old Testament* who has been based in Jerusalem and at Hong Kong Baptist University. He wrote a detailed critique, in a volume called *Studies in the Pentateuch*, of Mary Douglas's explanation of biblical dietary laws relative to respective classifications, divided by means of locomotion, which he argued against.

Michel Foucault (1926-1984) was a French philosopher, social theorist, and professor at Collège de France. He was chiefly interested in how power shapes knowledge and looked at social control in prisons and schools.

Sir James Frazer (1854-1941) was a Scottish social anthropologist* mainly associated with Trinity College, Cambridge. He is chiefly known for his book *The Golden Bough*, which examines common themes between ancient and modern religions, and argued that humanity progresses in order through magic, to religion, to science.

Sigmund Freud (1856-1939) was an Austrian Jewish neurologist and professor at the University of Vienna, who spent the end of his life in Britain after fleeing Nazi rule. He is considered the founder of psychoanalysis, in which clinicians treat psychological symptoms by attempting to probe patients' subconscious by discussing with them their ideas and memories.

Clifford Geertz (1926-2006) was an American anthropologist* and professor at the Institute for Advanced Study in Princeton. He was particularly drawn to decoding the symbolic content within rituals and art and is especially known for his concept of thick description* and his account of a Balinese cockfight.

Philip (P. H.) Gulliver is a Canadian anthropologist and distinguished research professor at York University who studied the Ndendeuli* people of Tanzania. In response to Mary Douglas, he argued there is in fact a very large number of traditional societies in which ideas of pollution do not actually play a large role.

Ian Hacking (b. 1936) is a now retired Canadian philosopher who specializes in the philosophy of science. He has taught at Cambridge University, Stanford University, the Collège de France, and the University of Toronto. He is known for his historical approach to the philosophy of science, and he reviewed many of Mary Douglas's books.

Marvin Harris (1927-2001) was an America anthropologist and professor at Columbia University and afterward the University of Florida. He viewed processes of production and demography as most important in understanding culture.

Walter Houston is a British Old Testament* scholar at Mansfield College, Oxford, and the University of Manchester. He applies anthropological theory regarding communal meals to understanding dietary rules in the book of Deuteronomy in the Torah and Old Testament*.

David Hume (1711-1776) was a Scottish historian, economist, and philosopher who was a significant influence in the British Enlightenment.* As an empiricist,* he believed all realities in the external world were the product of perception. He also was a skeptic regarding the limits of human knowledge and saw the human self as a bundle of perceptions.

Guillaume Iyenda is a sociologist in the United Kingdom who finished his PhD at Royal Holloway and also serves as secretary of the Lele* people in the United Kingdom. In this capacity, he delivered an address at Mary Douglas's funeral.

William James (1842-1910) was an American philosopher and physician, chiefly associated with Harvard, and one of the founders of psychology, particularly in the United States. In extensive writings on religion, he suggested academic work should focus on religious experience rather than institutions, and psychologists should also look to religious experience as a microscope of the mind.

Carl Jung (1875-1961) was a Swiss psychiatrist and psychoanalyst and student of Sigmund Freud, who split from his teacher and founded the approach of analytical psychology, looking into the lifelong psychological process of the development of the self (individuation).

Jesus of Nazareth (c. 4 B.C.E. – 30/33 C.E.) was a Jewish Galilean teacher, whose teachings are the foundation of Christianity.* Non-Christian contemporaneous sources, such as the Romano-Jewish historian Josephus and the Roman senator and historian Tacitus, provide independent attestations that Jesus was viewed broadly as a teacher and miracle worker before suffering a violent death by crucifixion.* Scholars generally regard Jesus's baptism, betrayal by a disciple, and crucifixion on orders of Pontius Pilate, Roman prefect of Judea, as historically probable.

Henri Lefebvre (1901–1991) was a French sociologist and philosopher who worked within the Marxist* tradition. He described what he saw as the social production of space and the concept of daily life, which under capitalism* encompasses zones of boredom mixed with promises of free time and leisure.

Claude Lévi-Strauss (1908–2009) held the chair of social anthropology* at the Collège de France and is often referred to as one of the parents of modern anthropology. He argued that so-called "savage" and "civilized" minds had the same structures and thought universal laws must produce similar myths in different cultures.

Michalis Lianos is a sociologist based in France at the Université de Rouen. He is particularly known for his work on fear and social control and the link in post-industrial societies between insecurity and otherness.

Max Liboiron is a geography professor in Canada at the Memorial University of Newfoundland. She is particularly interested in questions of waste and refuse and feminist approaches to understanding science.

Roland Littlewood (b. 1947) is professor of anthropology* and psychiatry at University College London and served between 1994 and 1997 as president of the Royal Anthropological Institute. He is especially interested in the overlap of medicine and anthropology in the Caribbean and Britain and in issues relating to diagnosis within the Caribbean immigrant population in Britain.

Moses Maimonides (1135/8-1204) was a medieval doctor and Jewish philosopher who was born in Spain and died in Egypt. His many influential works include *Guide for the Perplexed*, which seeks to reconcile Aristotelian philosophy with the theology of the Hebrew Bible by presenting rational explanations for the text.

Karl Marx (1818-1883) was a Prussian-born economist, sociologist, and journalist who spent much of his later life in London. He is particularly known for his three-volume *Das Kapital* (1867-1883) which introduces the field of political economy by its project of scientifically studying the effects of market capitalism on society.

Jacob Neusner (1932-2016) was an American scholar of Judaism* who for 20 years taught at Bard College. He translated most source texts of Rabbinic Judaism into English and was influential for treating them as works by their respective authors rather than a broad Rabbinic tradition.

Jerome Neyrey is a Jesuit theologian who completed his doctorate at Yale University and is now Professor of New Testament Studies at the University of Notre Dame. His study of the Gospel of Mark draws on the approaches of Mary Douglas in interpreting purity.

Friedrich Nietzsche (1844-1900) was a German philosopher and professor at the University of Basel who began his career examining Latin and Greek as preserved in classical texts. He is known for his critique of objective truth in favor of truth as observed from particular points of view, and his historical explanations for the rise of systems of morality, which he called genealogy.

Alfred Radcliffe-Brown (1881-1955) was a British social anthropologist,* and from 1937 to his retirement he held the first chair of social anthropology at Oxford. Greatly influenced by Émile Durkheim,* he developed the theories of structural functionalism* and coadaptation within British scholarship and founded the Institute of Social and Cultural Anthropology at Oxford, where Mary Douglas studied for her doctorate.

Richard Redding is an archaeology professor at the University of Michigan who researches the selective pressures that historically led societies to become more complex.

William Robertson Smith (1846-1894) was a Scottish Old Testament* scholar and clergyman who became professor of Arabic at Cambridge in 1889. He lost his position at the Aberdeen Free Church College in 1881 after accusations of heresy, prompted by his use of historical criticism in interpreting the Biblical texts.

Edward Sapir (1884-1939) was a Prussian-born anthropologist* and linguist who taught at the University of Chicago and Yale University. He was an early proponent of psychology's importation to anthropology, in the influence of individual personalities on the ultimate development of cultures and societies.

David Schneider (1918-1995) was an American cultural anthropologist who taught at the University of Chicago and after at the University of California, Santa Cruz. His fieldwork as a doctoral student at Harvard University was based in the Micronesian island of Yap,* and he later directed a Kinship Project at Chicago looking at how middle-class families in the United Kingdom and United States responded to kinship relations.

Joseph Schumpeter (1883-1950) was an Austrian-born economist and political scientist who served as Austria's finance minister in 1919 and, as a professor at Harvard University from 1932 until the end of his career, was one of the most important economists of his lifetime. Among his contributions was the concept of creative destruction.*

Jean Soler (b. 1933) is a French philosopher and writer who served as a diplomat at several of France's embassies overseas. In his writing he is especially interested in Old Testament* scholarship and the concept of monotheism.

Franz Steiner (1909-1952) was an ethnologist* and essayist born outside Prague and teaching at Oxford University as lecturer in social anthropology* from 1950 until his death. In his posthumously published lectures, he explained taboo as a concept whose essential function is of narrowing down and localizing danger.

Stanley Tambiah (1929-2014) was a Sri Lankan-born social anthropologist* who taught at Harvard University for most of his career and specialized in the anthropology* of religion along with societies of South East Asia.

Henry Temple, Third Viscount Palmerston (1784-1865) was British statesman who served twice as Prime Minister, from 1855-1858 and 1859-1865, and twice as Foreign Secretary, from 1835-841 and again from 1846-1851. His foreign policy would today be characterized as liberal interventionism, and along with the Liberal Party's first Prime Minister (from 1859), he remains the last British Prime Minister to die in office.

Victor Turner (1920-1983) was a Glasgow-born cultural anthropologist within the Manchester tradition of anthropology,* who spent much of his career beginning with his doctorate studying the Ndembu* tribe of Zambia. He spent his later life as a professor at the University of Chicago, where he looked at ritual as social dramas encapsulating both conflict and subsequent crisis resolution.

Gordon Wenham (b. 1943) is a British Old Testament* scholar who was senior professor of the Old Testament at the University of Gloucestershire from 1995 to 2005, and subsequently has lectured at Trinity College, Bristol. His books, on such subjects as the Book of Leviticus,* draw on Mary Douglas's concepts of holiness.

Aaron Wildavsky (1930-1993) was an American political scientist who chiefly worked at the University of California at Berkeley. He collaborated with Mary Douglas on the subject of how societies manage risk.

WORKS CITED

WORKS CITED

Campkin, Benjamin. "Placing 'Matter Out of Place': *Purity and Danger* as Evidence for Architecture and Urbanism." *Architectural Theory Review* 18, no. 1 (2013): 46-61.

Carrington, Damian. "Global Carbon Emissions Stood Still in 2016, Offering Climate Hope." *Guardian*, September 28, 2017. Accessed December 3, 2017. https://www.theguardian.com/environment/2017/sep/28/global-carbon-emissions-stood-still-in-2016-offering-climate-hope.

Clifford, Scott, and Dane G. Wendell. "How Disgust Influences Health Purity Attitudes." *Political Behavior* 38, no. 1 (2016): 155-178.

"Dame Mary Douglas." *Telegraph.* May 22, 2007. Accessed December 3, 2017. http://www.telegraph.co.uk/news/obituaries/1552231/Dame-Mary-Douglas.html.

Douglas, Mary. *Purity and Danger: An Analysis of Concepts of Pollution and Taboo.* Vol. 2 of *Mary Douglas: Collected Works.* Abingdon: Routledge, 2002.

"Atonement in Leviticus." *Jewish Studies Quarterly* 1.2 (1993/4): 109-130.

Implicit Meanings: Essays in Anthropology. London: Routledge & Kegan Paul, 1975.

"The Glorious Book of Numbers," *Jewish Studies Quarterly* 1.3 (1993/4): 193-216.

"The Stranger in the Bible," *Archives Européennes de Sociologie* 35.1 (1994): 283-298.

Leviticus as Literature. Oxford: Oxford University Press, 1999.

"Sorcery Accusations Unleashed: The Lele Revisited, 1987." *Africa: Journal of the International African Institute,* 69, no. 2 (1999): 177-193.

Dominian, Jack. Review of *Purity and Danger*. *New Blackfriars* 48, no. 557 (October 1966): 47-48.

Durkheim, Émile. *The Division of Labor in Society,* W. D. Halls trans. New York: Free Press, 1997.

Eliade, Mircea. *Shamanism: Archaic Techniques of Ecstasy*. 1951. Willard Trask trans. Princeton, N.J.: Princeton University Press, 2004.

Eriksen, Thomas Hyllan, and Finn Sivert Nielsen. *A History of Anthropology*. London: Pluto Press, 2013.

Fardon, Richard. "Dame Mary Douglas." Guardian, May 18, 2007. Accessed December 3, 2017. https://www.theguardian.com/news/2007/may/18/guardianobituaries.obituaries.

Firmage, Edwin. "The Biblical Dietary Laws and the Concept of Holiness." In J.A. Emerton, *Studies in the Pentateuch.* Leiden: E.J. Brill, 1990.

Frazer, James George, *The Golden Bough. A Study in Magic and Religion. Part 1: The Magic Art and the Evolution of Kings, Vol. 1.* London: The Macmillan Press. [1906] 1976.

Guilford, Gwynn. "China's Mountains of Garbage." *The Atlantic*, March 25, 2013. Accessed December 3, 2017. https://www.theatlantic.com/china/archive/2013/03/chinas-mountains-of-garbage/274329/.

Gulliver, P. H. Review of *Purity and Danger. Bulletin of the School of Oriental and African Studies* 30, no. 2 (1967): 462-464.

Hacking, Ian. "Risk and Dirt." In *Risk and Morality.* Toronto: University of Toronto Press, 2003.

Houston, Walter. *Purity and Monotheism: Clean and Unclean Animals in Biblical Law.* Sheffield: JSOT Press, 1993.

Inbar, Yoel, David Pizarro, Ravi Iyer and Jonathan Haidt. "Disgust Sensitivity, Political Conservatism, and Voting." *Social Psychological and Personality Science* 3 (2012): 537.

Jackson, Lee. *Dirty Old London: The Victorian Fight Against Filth.* New Haven: Yale University Press, 2014.

Heft, J. L., ed. *Believing Scholars: Ten Catholic Intellectuals*. New York: Fordham Univ. Press, 2005.

Liboiron, Max. "Discard Studies as Science and Technology Studies (STS)" (blog). *Discard Studies*. October 16, 2013. Accessed December 3, 2017. https://discardstudies.com/2013/10/16/discard-studies-as-science-and-technology-studies-sts/.

Littlewood, Roland. "Degrees of Mastery in the Work of Mary Douglas." *Anthropology Today*, 14, no. 6 (December 1998): 1-2.

Luhrmann, Tanya. "The Paradox of Donald Trump's Appeal." *Sapiens*, July 29, 2016. Accessed December 3, 2017. https://www.sapiens.org/culture/mary-douglas-donald-trump/.

McGreevy, John. "Mary Douglas RIP." *Commonweal*, May 22, 2007. Accessed December 3, 2017. https://www.commonwealmagazine.org/mary-douglas-rip.

Neusner, Jacob. *Idea of Purity in Ancient Judaism.* Leiden and Boston: Brill Academic Publishers, 1973.

Perri, 6, ed. *The Institutional Dynamics of Culture: The New Durkheimians. Farnham, UK: Ashgate, 2008.*

"Professor Dame Mary Douglas, 1921-2007." *The Douglas Archives.* Accessed December 3, 2017. *http://www.douglashistory.co.uk/history/marydouglas2.htm.*

Redding, Richard W. "The Pig and the Chicken in the Middle East: Modeling Human Subsistence Behavior in the Archaeological Record Using Historical and Animal Husbandry Data." Journal of Archaeological Research 23, no. 4 (13 March 2015): 325.

Scott, J. ed. Fifty Key Sociologists: The Contemporary Theorists. London: Routledge, 2007.

Tyler, Edward Burnett. Primitive Culture: Research into the Development of Mythology, Philosophy, Religion, Art, and Custom. London: John Murray, 1871.

Welbourn. F. B. "Mary Douglas and the Study of Religion." *Journal of Religion in Africa*, 3, no. 1 (1970): 89-95.

Yiu, Pak. "China Ban on Waste Imports Leads to Piles of Paper Abroad, Surging Prices in China," Reuters, September 28, 2017, accessed January 20, 2017, https://www.reuters.com/article/us-china-hongkong-paperrecycling/china-ban-on-waste-imports-leads-to-piles-of-paper-abroad-surging-prices-in-china-idUSKCN1C30GR.

THE MACAT LIBRARY
BY DISCIPLINE

AFRICANA STUDIES

Chinua Achebe's *An Image of Africa: Racism in Conrad's Heart of Darkness*
W. E. B. Du Bois's *The Souls of Black Folk*
Zora Neale Huston's *Characteristics of Negro Expression*
Martin Luther King Jr's *Why We Can't Wait*
Toni Morrison's *Playing in the Dark: Whiteness in the American Literary Imagination*

ANTHROPOLOGY

Arjun Appadurai's *Modernity at Large: Cultural Dimensions of Globalisation*
Philippe Ariès's *Centuries of Childhood*
Franz Boas's *Race, Language and Culture*
Kim Chan & Renée Mauborgne's *Blue Ocean Strategy*
Jared Diamond's *Guns, Germs & Steel: the Fate of Human Societies*
Jared Diamond's *Collapse: How Societies Choose to Fail or Survive*
E. E. Evans-Pritchard's *Witchcraft, Oracles and Magic Among the Azande*
James Ferguson's *The Anti-Politics Machine*
Clifford Geertz's *The Interpretation of Cultures*
David Graeber's *Debt: the First 5000 Years*
Karen Ho's *Liquidated: An Ethnography of Wall Street*
Geert Hofstede's *Culture's Consequences: Comparing Values, Behaviors, Institutes and Organizations across Nations*
Claude Lévi-Strauss's *Structural Anthropology*
Jay Macleod's *Ain't No Makin' It: Aspirations and Attainment in a Low-Income Neighborhood*
Saba Mahmood's *The Politics of Piety: The Islamic Revival and the Feminist Subject*
Marcel Mauss's *The Gift*

BUSINESS

Jean Lave & Etienne Wenger's *Situated Learning*
Theodore Levitt's *Marketing Myopia*
Burton G. Malkiel's *A Random Walk Down Wall Street*
Douglas McGregor's *The Human Side of Enterprise*
Michael Porter's *Competitive Strategy: Creating and Sustaining Superior Performance*
John Kotter's *Leading Change*
C. K. Prahalad & Gary Hamel's *The Core Competence of the Corporation*

CRIMINOLOGY

Michelle Alexander's *The New Jim Crow: Mass Incarceration in the Age of Colorblindness*
Michael R. Gottfredson & Travis Hirschi's *A General Theory of Crime*
Richard Herrnstein & Charles A. Murray's *The Bell Curve: Intelligence and Class Structure in American Life*
Elizabeth Loftus's *Eyewitness Testimony*
Jay Macleod's *Ain't No Makin' It: Aspirations and Attainment in a Low-Income Neighborhood*
Philip Zimbardo's *The Lucifer Effect*

ECONOMICS

Janet Abu-Lughod's *Before European Hegemony*
Ha-Joon Chang's *Kicking Away the Ladder*
David Brion Davis's *The Problem of Slavery in the Age of Revolution*
Milton Friedman's *The Role of Monetary Policy*
Milton Friedman's *Capitalism and Freedom*
David Graeber's *Debt: the First 5000 Years*
Friedrich Hayek's *The Road to Serfdom*
Karen Ho's *Liquidated: An Ethnography of Wall Street*

John Maynard Keynes's *The General Theory of Employment, Interest and Money*
Charles P. Kindleberger's *Manias, Panics and Crashes*
Robert Lucas's *Why Doesn't Capital Flow from Rich to Poor Countries?*
Burton G. Malkiel's *A Random Walk Down Wall Street*
Thomas Robert Malthus's *An Essay on the Principle of Population*
Karl Marx's *Capital*
Thomas Piketty's *Capital in the Twenty-First Century*
Amartya Sen's *Development as Freedom*
Adam Smith's *The Wealth of Nations*
Nassim Nicholas Taleb's *The Black Swan: The Impact of the Highly Improbable*
Amos Tversky's & Daniel Kahneman's *Judgment under Uncertainty: Heuristics and Biases*
Mahbub Ul Haq's *Reflections on Human Development*
Max Weber's *The Protestant Ethic and the Spirit of Capitalism*

FEMINISM AND GENDER STUDIES

Judith Butler's *Gender Trouble*
Simone De Beauvoir's *The Second Sex*
Michel Foucault's *History of Sexuality*
Betty Friedan's *The Feminine Mystique*
Saba Mahmood's *The Politics of Piety: The Islamic Revival and the Feminist Subject*
Joan Wallach Scott's *Gender and the Politics of History*
Mary Wollstonecraft's *A Vindication of the Rights of Women*
Virginia Woolf's *A Room of One's Own*

GEOGRAPHY

The Brundtland Report's *Our Common Future*
Rachel Carson's *Silent Spring*
Charles Darwin's *On the Origin of Species*
James Ferguson's *The Anti-Politics Machine*
Jane Jacobs's *The Death and Life of Great American Cities*
James Lovelock's *Gaia: A New Look at Life on Earth*
Amartya Sen's *Development as Freedom*
Mathis Wackernagel & William Rees's *Our Ecological Footprint*

HISTORY

Janet Abu-Lughod's *Before European Hegemony*
Benedict Anderson's *Imagined Communities*
Bernard Bailyn's *The Ideological Origins of the American Revolution*
Hanna Batatu's *The Old Social Classes And The Revolutionary Movements Of Iraq*
Christopher Browning's *Ordinary Men: Reserve Police Batallion 101 and the Final Solution in Poland*
Edmund Burke's *Reflections on the Revolution in France*
William Cronon's *Nature's Metropolis: Chicago And The Great West*
Alfred W. Crosby's *The Columbian Exchange*
Hamid Dabashi's *Iran: A People Interrupted*
David Brion Davis's *The Problem of Slavery in the Age of Revolution*
Nathalie Zemon Davis's *The Return of Martin Guerre*
Jared Diamond's *Guns, Germs & Steel: the Fate of Human Societies*
Frank Dikotter's *Mao's Great Famine*
John W Dower's *War Without Mercy: Race And Power In The Pacific War*
W. E. B. Du Bois's *The Souls of Black Folk*
Richard J. Evans's *In Defence of History*
Lucien Febvre's *The Problem of Unbelief in the 16th Century*
Sheila Fitzpatrick's *Everyday Stalinism*

The Macat Library By Discipline

Eric Foner's *Reconstruction: America's Unfinished Revolution, 1863-1877*
Michel Foucault's *Discipline and Punish*
Michel Foucault's *History of Sexuality*
Francis Fukuyama's *The End of History and the Last Man*
John Lewis Gaddis's *We Now Know: Rethinking Cold War History*
Ernest Gellner's *Nations and Nationalism*
Eugene Genovese's *Roll, Jordan, Roll: The World the Slaves Made*
Carlo Ginzburg's *The Night Battles*
Daniel Goldhagen's *Hitler's Willing Executioners*
Jack Goldstone's *Revolution and Rebellion in the Early Modern World*
Antonio Gramsci's *The Prison Notebooks*
Alexander Hamilton, John Jay & James Madison's *The Federalist Papers*
Christopher Hill's *The World Turned Upside Down*
Carole Hillenbrand's *The Crusades: Islamic Perspectives*
Thomas Hobbes's *Leviathan*
Eric Hobsbawm's *The Age Of Revolution*
John A. Hobson's *Imperialism: A Study*
Albert Hourani's *History of the Arab Peoples*
Samuel P. Huntington's *The Clash of Civilizations and the Remaking of World Order*
C. L. R. James's *The Black Jacobins*
Tony Judt's *Postwar: A History of Europe Since 1945*
Ernst Kantorowicz's *The King's Two Bodies: A Study in Medieval Political Theology*
Paul Kennedy's *The Rise and Fall of the Great Powers*
Ian Kershaw's *The "Hitler Myth": Image and Reality in the Third Reich*
John Maynard Keynes's *The General Theory of Employment, Interest and Money*
Charles P. Kindleberger's *Manias, Panics and Crashes*
Martin Luther King Jr's *Why We Can't Wait*
Henry Kissinger's *World Order: Reflections on the Character of Nations and the Course of History*
Thomas Kuhn's *The Structure of Scientific Revolutions*
Georges Lefebvre's *The Coming of the French Revolution*
John Locke's *Two Treatises of Government*
Niccolò Machiavelli's *The Prince*
Thomas Robert Malthus's *An Essay on the Principle of Population*
Mahmood Mamdani's *Citizen and Subject: Contemporary Africa And The Legacy Of Late Colonialism*
Karl Marx's *Capital*
Stanley Milgram's *Obedience to Authority*
John Stuart Mill's *On Liberty*
Thomas Paine's *Common Sense*
Thomas Paine's *Rights of Man*
Geoffrey Parker's *Global Crisis: War, Climate Change and Catastrophe in the Seventeenth Century*
Jonathan Riley-Smith's *The First Crusade and the Idea of Crusading*
Jean-Jacques Rousseau's *The Social Contract*
Joan Wallach Scott's *Gender and the Politics of History*
Theda Skocpol's *States and Social Revolutions*
Adam Smith's *The Wealth of Nations*
Timothy Snyder's *Bloodlands: Europe Between Hitler and Stalin*
Sun Tzu's *The Art of War*
Keith Thomas's *Religion and the Decline of Magic*
Thucydides's *The History of the Peloponnesian War*
Frederick Jackson Turner's *The Significance of the Frontier in American History*
Odd Arne Westad's *The Global Cold War: Third World Interventions And The Making Of Our Times*

LITERATURE

Chinua Achebe's *An Image of Africa: Racism in Conrad's Heart of Darkness*
Roland Barthes's *Mythologies*
Homi K. Bhabha's *The Location of Culture*
Judith Butler's *Gender Trouble*
Simone De Beauvoir's *The Second Sex*
Ferdinand De Saussure's *Course in General Linguistics*
T. S. Eliot's *The Sacred Wood: Essays on Poetry and Criticism*
Zora Neale Huston's *Characteristics of Negro Expression*
Toni Morrison's *Playing in the Dark: Whiteness in the American Literary Imagination*
Edward Said's *Orientalism*
Gayatri Chakravorty Spivak's *Can the Subaltern Speak?*
Mary Wollstonecraft's *A Vindication of the Rights of Women*
Virginia Woolf's *A Room of One's Own*

PHILOSOPHY

Elizabeth Anscombe's *Modern Moral Philosophy*
Hannah Arendt's *The Human Condition*
Aristotle's *Metaphysics*
Aristotle's *Nicomachean Ethics*
Edmund Gettier's *Is Justified True Belief Knowledge?*
Georg Wilhelm Friedrich Hegel's *Phenomenology of Spirit*
David Hume's *Dialogues Concerning Natural Religion*
David Hume's *The Enquiry for Human Understanding*
Immanuel Kant's *Religion within the Boundaries of Mere Reason*
Immanuel Kant's *Critique of Pure Reason*
Søren Kierkegaard's *The Sickness Unto Death*
Søren Kierkegaard's *Fear and Trembling*
C. S. Lewis's *The Abolition of Man*
Alasdair MacIntyre's *After Virtue*
Marcus Aurelius's *Meditations*
Friedrich Nietzsche's *On the Genealogy of Morality*
Friedrich Nietzsche's *Beyond Good and Evil*
Plato's *Republic*
Plato's *Symposium*
Jean-Jacques Rousseau's *The Social Contract*
Gilbert Ryle's *The Concept of Mind*
Baruch Spinoza's *Ethics*
Sun Tzu's *The Art of War*
Ludwig Wittgenstein's *Philosophical Investigations*

POLITICS

Benedict Anderson's *Imagined Communities*
Aristotle's *Politics*
Bernard Bailyn's *The Ideological Origins of the American Revolution*
Edmund Burke's *Reflections on the Revolution in France*
John C. Calhoun's *A Disquisition on Government*
Ha-Joon Chang's *Kicking Away the Ladder*
Hamid Dabashi's *Iran: A People Interrupted*
Hamid Dabashi's *Theology of Discontent: The Ideological Foundation of the Islamic Revolution in Iran*
Robert Dahl's *Democracy and its Critics*
Robert Dahl's *Who Governs?*
David Brion Davis's *The Problem of Slavery in the Age of Revolution*

The Macat Library By Discipline

Alexis De Tocqueville's *Democracy in America*
James Ferguson's *The Anti-Politics Machine*
Frank Dikotter's *Mao's Great Famine*
Sheila Fitzpatrick's *Everyday Stalinism*
Eric Foner's *Reconstruction: America's Unfinished Revolution, 1863-1877*
Milton Friedman's *Capitalism and Freedom*
Francis Fukuyama's *The End of History and the Last Man*
John Lewis Gaddis's *We Now Know: Rethinking Cold War History*
Ernest Gellner's *Nations and Nationalism*
David Graeber's *Debt: the First 5000 Years*
Antonio Gramsci's *The Prison Notebooks*
Alexander Hamilton, John Jay & James Madison's *The Federalist Papers*
Friedrich Hayek's *The Road to Serfdom*
Christopher Hill's *The World Turned Upside Down*
Thomas Hobbes's *Leviathan*
John A. Hobson's *Imperialism: A Study*
Samuel P. Huntington's *The Clash of Civilizations and the Remaking of World Order*
Tony Judt's *Postwar: A History of Europe Since 1945*
David C. Kang's *China Rising: Peace, Power and Order in East Asia*
Paul Kennedy's *The Rise and Fall of Great Powers*
Robert Keohane's *After Hegemony*
Martin Luther King Jr.'s *Why We Can't Wait*
Henry Kissinger's *World Order: Reflections on the Character of Nations and the Course of History*
John Locke's *Two Treatises of Government*
Niccolò Machiavelli's *The Prince*
Thomas Robert Malthus's *An Essay on the Principle of Population*
Mahmood Mamdani's *Citizen and Subject: Contemporary Africa And The Legacy Of Late Colonialism*
Karl Marx's *Capital*
John Stuart Mill's *On Liberty*
John Stuart Mill's *Utilitarianism*
Hans Morgenthau's *Politics Among Nations*
Thomas Paine's *Common Sense*
Thomas Paine's *Rights of Man*
Thomas Piketty's *Capital in the Twenty-First Century*
Robert D. Putman's *Bowling Alone*
John Rawls's *Theory of Justice*
Jean-Jacques Rousseau's *The Social Contract*
Theda Skocpol's *States and Social Revolutions*
Adam Smith's *The Wealth of Nations*
Sun Tzu's *The Art of War*
Henry David Thoreau's *Civil Disobedience*
Thucydides's *The History of the Peloponnesian War*
Kenneth Waltz's *Theory of International Politics*
Max Weber's *Politics as a Vocation*
Odd Arne Westad's *The Global Cold War: Third World Interventions And The Making Of Our Times*

POSTCOLONIAL STUDIES

Roland Barthes's *Mythologies*
Frantz Fanon's *Black Skin, White Masks*
Homi K. Bhabha's *The Location of Culture*
Gustavo Gutiérrez's *A Theology of Liberation*
Edward Said's *Orientalism*
Gayatri Chakravorty Spivak's *Can the Subaltern Speak?*

PSYCHOLOGY

Gordon Allport's *The Nature of Prejudice*
Alan Baddeley & Graham Hitch's *Aggression: A Social Learning Analysis*
Albert Bandura's *Aggression: A Social Learning Analysis*
Leon Festinger's *A Theory of Cognitive Dissonance*
Sigmund Freud's *The Interpretation of Dreams*
Betty Friedan's *The Feminine Mystique*
Michael R. Gottfredson & Travis Hirschi's *A General Theory of Crime*
Eric Hoffer's *The True Believer: Thoughts on the Nature of Mass Movements*
William James's *Principles of Psychology*
Elizabeth Loftus's *Eyewitness Testimony*
A. H. Maslow's *A Theory of Human Motivation*
Stanley Milgram's *Obedience to Authority*
Steven Pinker's *The Better Angels of Our Nature*
Oliver Sacks's *The Man Who Mistook His Wife For a Hat*
Richard Thaler & Cass Sunstein's *Nudge: Improving Decisions About Health, Wealth and Happiness*
Amos Tversky's *Judgment under Uncertainty: Heuristics and Biases*
Philip Zimbardo's *The Lucifer Effect*

SCIENCE

Rachel Carson's *Silent Spring*
William Cronon's *Nature's Metropolis: Chicago And The Great West*
Alfred W. Crosby's *The Columbian Exchange*
Charles Darwin's *On the Origin of Species*
Richard Dawkin's *The Selfish Gene*
Thomas Kuhn's *The Structure of Scientific Revolutions*
Geoffrey Parker's *Global Crisis: War, Climate Change and Catastrophe in the Seventeenth Century*
Mathis Wackernagel & William Rees's *Our Ecological Footprint*

SOCIOLOGY

Michelle Alexander's *The New Jim Crow: Mass Incarceration in the Age of Colorblindness*
Gordon Allport's *The Nature of Prejudice*
Albert Bandura's *Aggression: A Social Learning Analysis*
Hanna Batatu's *The Old Social Classes And The Revolutionary Movements Of Iraq*
Ha-Joon Chang's *Kicking Away the Ladder*
W. E. B. Du Bois's *The Souls of Black Folk*
Émile Durkheim's *On Suicide*
Frantz Fanon's *Black Skin, White Masks*
Frantz Fanon's *The Wretched of the Earth*
Eric Foner's *Reconstruction: America's Unfinished Revolution, 1863-1877*
Eugene Genovese's *Roll, Jordan, Roll: The World the Slaves Made*
Jack Goldstone's *Revolution and Rebellion in the Early Modern World*
Antonio Gramsci's *The Prison Notebooks*
Richard Herrnstein & Charles A Murray's *The Bell Curve: Intelligence and Class Structure in American Life*
Eric Hoffer's *The True Believer: Thoughts on the Nature of Mass Movements*
Jane Jacobs's *The Death and Life of Great American Cities*
Robert Lucas's *Why Doesn't Capital Flow from Rich to Poor Countries?*
Jay Macleod's *Ain't No Makin' It: Aspirations and Attainment in a Low Income Neighborhood*
Elaine May's *Homeward Bound: American Families in the Cold War Era*
Douglas McGregor's *The Human Side of Enterprise*
C. Wright Mills's *The Sociological Imagination*

The Macat Library By Discipline

Thomas Piketty's *Capital in the Twenty-First Century*
Robert D. Putman's *Bowling Alone*
David Riesman's *The Lonely Crowd: A Study of the Changing American Character*
Edward Said's *Orientalism*
Joan Wallach Scott's *Gender and the Politics of History*
Theda Skocpol's *States and Social Revolutions*
Max Weber's *The Protestant Ethic and the Spirit of Capitalism*

THEOLOGY

Augustine's *Confessions*
Benedict's *Rule of St Benedict*
Gustavo Gutiérrez's *A Theology of Liberation*
Carole Hillenbrand's *The Crusades: Islamic Perspectives*
David Hume's *Dialogues Concerning Natural Religion*
Immanuel Kant's *Religion within the Boundaries of Mere Reason*
Ernst Kantorowicz's *The King's Two Bodies: A Study in Medieval Political Theology*
Søren Kierkegaard's *The Sickness Unto Death*
C. S. Lewis's *The Abolition of Man*
Saba Mahmood's *The Politics of Piety: The Islamic Revival and the Feminist Subject*
Baruch Spinoza's *Ethics*
Keith Thomas's *Religion and the Decline of Magic*

COMING SOON

Chris Argyris's *The Individual and the Organisation*
Seyla Benhabib's *The Rights of Others*
Walter Benjamin's *The Work Of Art in the Age of Mechanical Reproduction*
John Berger's *Ways of Seeing*
Pierre Bourdieu's *Outline of a Theory of Practice*
Mary Douglas's *Purity and Danger*
Roland Dworkin's *Taking Rights Seriously*
James G. March's *Exploration and Exploitation in Organisational Learning*
Ikujiro Nonaka's *A Dynamic Theory of Organizational Knowledge Creation*
Griselda Pollock's *Vision and Difference*
Amartya Sen's *Inequality Re-Examined*
Susan Sontag's *On Photography*
Yasser Tabbaa's *The Transformation of Islamic Art*
Ludwig von Mises's *Theory of Money and Credit*

Macat Disciplines

Access the greatest ideas and thinkers across entire disciplines, including

Postcolonial Studies

Roland Barthes's *Mythologies*
Frantz Fanon's *Black Skin, White Masks*
Homi K. Bhabha's *The Location of Culture*
Gustavo Gutiérrez's *A Theology of Liberation*
Edward Said's *Orientalism*
Gayatri Chakravorty Spivak's *Can the Subaltern Speak?*

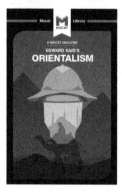

Macat analyses are available from all good bookshops and libraries.

Access hundreds of analyses through one, multimedia tool.
Join free for one month **library.macat.com**

Macat Disciplines

Access the greatest ideas and thinkers across entire disciplines, including

AFRICANA STUDIES

Chinua Achebe's *An Image of Africa: Racism in Conrad's Heart of Darkness*

W. E. B. Du Bois's *The Souls of Black Folk*

Zora Neale Hurston's *Characteristics of Negro Expression*

Martin Luther King Jr.'s *Why We Can't Wait*

Toni Morrison's *Playing in the Dark: Whiteness in the American Literary Imagination*

Macat Disciplines

Access the greatest ideas and thinkers across entire disciplines, including

FEMINISM, GENDER AND QUEER STUDIES

Simone De Beauvoir's
The Second Sex

Michel Foucault's
History of Sexuality

Betty Friedan's
The Feminine Mystique

Saba Mahmood's
*The Politics of Piety:
The Islamic Revival and
the Feminist Subject*

Joan Wallach Scott's
*Gender and the
Politics of History*

Mary Wollstonecraft's
*A Vindication of the
Rights of Woman*

Virginia Woolf's
A Room of One's Own

Judith Butler's
Gender Trouble

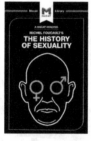

Macat Disciplines

Access the greatest ideas and thinkers across entire disciplines, including

CRIMINOLOGY

Michelle Alexander's
The New Jim Crow:
Mass Incarceration in the
Age of Colorblindness

Michael R. Gottfredson
& Travis Hirschi's
A General Theory of Crime

Elizabeth Loftus's
Eyewitness Testimony

Richard Herrnstein
& Charles A. Murray's
The Bell Curve: Intelligence and
Class Structure in American Life

Jay Macleod's
Ain't No Makin' It:
Aspirations and Attainment in a
Low-Income Neighborhood

Philip Zimbardo's
The Lucifer Effect

Macat Disciplines

Access the greatest ideas and thinkers across entire disciplines, including

INEQUALITY

Ha-Joon Chang's, *Kicking Away the Ladder*

David Graeber's, *Debt: The First 5000 Years*

Robert E. Lucas's, *Why Doesn't Capital Flow from Rich To Poor Countries?*

Thomas Piketty's, *Capital in the Twenty-First Century*

Amartya Sen's, *Inequality Re-Examined*

Mahbub Ul Haq's, *Reflections on Human Development*

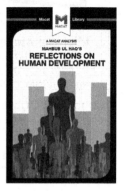

Macat analyses are available from all good bookshops and libraries.

Access hundreds of analyses through one, multimedia tool.
Join free for one month **library.macat.com**

Macat Disciplines

Access the greatest ideas and thinkers across entire disciplines, including

GLOBALIZATION

Arjun Appadurai's, *Modernity at Large: Cultural Dimensions of Globalisation*

James Ferguson's, *The Anti-Politics Machine*

Geert Hofstede's, *Culture's Consequences*

Amartya Sen's, *Development as Freedom*

Macat Disciplines

Access the greatest ideas and thinkers across entire disciplines, including

MAN AND THE ENVIRONMENT

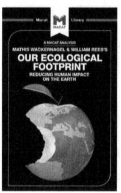

The Brundtland Report's, *Our Common Future*
Rachel Carson's, *Silent Spring*
James Lovelock's, *Gaia: A New Look at Life on Earth*
Mathis Wackernagel & William Rees's, *Our Ecological Footprint*

Macat analyses are available from all good bookshops and libraries.

Access hundreds of analyses through one, multimedia tool.
Join free for one month **library.macat.com**

Macat Disciplines

*Access the greatest ideas and thinkers
across entire disciplines, including*

THE FUTURE OF DEMOCRACY

Robert A. Dahl's, *Democracy and Its Critics*
Robert A. Dahl's, *Who Governs?*
Alexis De Toqueville's, *Democracy in America*
Niccolò Machiavelli's, *The Prince*
John Stuart Mill's, *On Liberty*
Robert D. Putnam's, *Bowling Alone*
Jean-Jacques Rousseau's, *The Social Contract*
Henry David Thoreau's, *Civil Disobedience*

Macat Disciplines

Access the greatest ideas and thinkers across entire disciplines, including

TOTALITARIANISM

Sheila Fitzpatrick's, *Everyday Stalinism*
Ian Kershaw's, *The "Hitler Myth"*
Timothy Snyder's, *Bloodlands*

Macat analyses are available from all good bookshops and libraries.

Access hundreds of analyses through one, multimedia tool.
Join free for one month **library.macat.com**

Macat Pairs

Analyse historical and modern issues from opposite sides of an argument. Pairs include:

RACE AND IDENTITY

Zora Neale Hurston's
Characteristics of Negro Expression

Using material collected on anthropological expeditions to the South, Zora Neale Hurston explains how expression in African American culture in the early twentieth century departs from the art of white America. At the time, African American art was often criticized for copying white culture. For Hurston, this criticism misunderstood how art works. European tradition views art as something fixed. But Hurston describes a creative process that is alive, ever-changing, and largely improvisational. She maintains that African American art works through a process called 'mimicry'—where an imitated object or verbal pattern, for example, is reshaped and altered until it becomes something new, novel—and worthy of attention.

Frantz Fanon's
Black Skin, White Masks

Black Skin, White Masks offers a radical analysis of the psychological effects of colonization on the colonized.

Fanon witnessed the effects of colonization first hand both in his birthplace, Martinique, and again later in life when he worked as a psychiatrist in another French colony, Algeria. His text is uncompromising in form and argument. He dissects the dehumanizing effects of colonialism, arguing that it destroys the native sense of identity, forcing people to adapt to an alien set of values—including a core belief that they are inferior. This results in deep psychological trauma.

Fanon's work played a pivotal role in the civil rights movements of the 1960s.

Macat analyses are available from all good bookshops and libraries.

Access hundreds of analyses through one, multimedia tool.
Join free for one month **library.macat.com**

Macat Pairs

Analyse historical and modern issues from opposite sides of an argument. Pairs include:

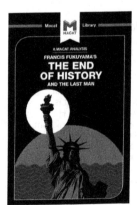

Macat Pairs

Analyse historical and modern issues from opposite sides of an argument. Pairs include:

HOW TO RUN AN ECONOMY

John Maynard Keynes's
The General Theory OF Employment, Interest and Money

Classical economics suggests that market economies are self-correcting in times of recession or depression, and tend toward full employment and output. But English economist John Maynard Keynes disagrees.

In his ground-breaking 1936 study *The General Theory*, Keynes argues that traditional economics has misunderstood the causes of unemployment. Employment is not determined by the price of labor; it is directly linked to demand. Keynes believes market economies are by nature unstable, and so require government intervention. Spurred on by the social catastrophe of the Great Depression of the 1930s, he sets out to revolutionize the way the world thinks

Milton Friedman's
The Role of Monetary Policy

Friedman's 1968 paper changed the course of economic theory. In just 17 pages, he demolished existing theory and outlined an effective alternate monetary policy designed to secure 'high employment, stable prices and rapid growth.'

Friedman demonstrated that monetary policy plays a vital role in broader economic stability and argued that economists got their monetary policy wrong in the 1950s and 1960s by misunderstanding the relationship between inflation and unemployment. Previous generations of economists had believed that governments could permanently decrease unemployment by permitting inflation—and vice versa. Friedman's most original contribution was to show that this supposed trade-off is an illusion that only works in the short term.

Macat analyses are available from all good bookshops and libraries.

Access hundreds of analyses through one, multimedia tool.
Join free for one month **library.macat.com**

Printed in the United States
by Baker & Taylor Publisher Services